Loss

Loss of Innocence,
Loss of Shame,
Loss of Fortune,
Loss of Fame.

Loss of Focus,
Loss of Scope,
Loss of Purpose,
Loss of Hope.

Loss of Meaning,
Loss of Means,
Loss of Goals,
Loss of Dreams.

Loss of Substance,
Loss of Source,
Loss of Relevance,
Loss of Force.

Loss of Memory,
Loss of Time,
Loss of Rhythm,
Loss of Rhyme.

Loss of Power,
Loss of Funds,
Loss of Daughters,
Loss of Sons.

Loss of Direction,
Loss of Self,
Loss of Perspectives,
Loss of Health.

Loss Is Something,
We All Face,
As Members of
This Human Race.

Verline Gee-Fleming (Alex Gee's mother)

WHEN

GOD

LETS

YOU

DOWN

Trusting Again After Pain and Loss

ALEX GEE

IVP Books

An imprint of InterVarsity Press
Downers Grove, Illinois

InterVarsity Press
P.O. Box 1400, Downers Grove, IL 60515-1426
World Wide Web: www.ivpress.com
E-mail: email@ivpress.com

InterVarsity Press® is the book-publishing division of InterVarsity Christian Fellowship/USA®, a student movement active on campus at hundreds of universities, colleges and schools of nursing in the United States of America, and a member movement of the International Fellowship of Evangelical Students. For information about local and regional activities, write Public Relations Dept., InterVarsity Christian Fellowship/USA, 6400 Schroeder Rd., P.O. Box 7895, Madison, WI 53707-7895, or visit the IVCF website at <www.intervarsity.org>.

All Scripture quotations, unless otherwise indicated, are taken from the Holy Bible, New International Version®. NIV®. Copyright ©1973, 1978, 1984 by International Bible Society. *Used by permission of Zondervan Publishing House. All rights reserved.*

Design: Cindy Kiple
Images: Lynn James/Getty Images

ISBN-10: 0-8308-3397-8
ISBN-13: 978-0-8308-3397-9

Printed in the United States of America ∞

Library of Congress Cataloging-in-Publication Data

Gee, Alex, 1963-
    When God lets you down: trusting again after pain and loss/
    Alex Gee
      p. cm.
    ISBN-13: 978-0-8308-3397-9 (pbk.: alk. paper)
    ISBN-10: 0-8308-3397-8 (pbk.: alk. paper)
    1. Trust in God—Christianity.   2. Suffering—Religious aspects
—Christianity.   3. Hope—Religious aspects—Christianity.   I.
Title. BV4637.G44 2006 248.8'6—dc22
                    2006020899

| P | 19 | 18 | 17 | 16 | 15 | 14 | 13 | 12 | 11 | 10 | 9 | 8 | 7 | 6 | 5 | 4 | 3 | 2 | 1 |
| Y | 21 | 20 | 19 | 18 | 17 | 16 | 15 | 14 | 13 | 12 | 11 | 10 | 09 | 08 | 07 | 06 | | | | |

This book is dedicated to all those who,

because of tragedy and disappointment,

find themselves far from the peace and joy of the Holy Spirit,

yet they long to trust in God's goodness again.

This book is also dedicated to the memory

of our prematurely born daughters,

Victoria and Alexis.

CONTENTS

FOREWORD

The phone rang and interrupted the peaceful beginning of my Thanksgiving Day 1996. It was my friend Alex, and I thought he was calling to wish me a happy holiday. But the first sentences drove a stake of pain through my heart. "Something is wrong! Jackie is bleeding and may be in labor! We're on our way to the hospital!" I was looking forward to a phone call about an impending birth—in March or so—but this was only late November.

"I'll meet you there," was all I could say.

I hung up the phone and began to cry. I was flooded with the memories of all the talks that Alex and I had had over the past several years.

We were introduced about the time that Alex and Jackie had lost their second baby daughter. Shortly thereafter we began to meet every Thursday morning for breakfast. I had no idea at the time what was really going on in the heart of this bright, young, gifted African American pastor with such a growing reputation in the city. I was just thankful that he was willing to meet with me, a middle-aged white guy whose background could not have been any more different from his. I had grown up in the rural Northwest, the child of a stable home, in a Lutheran church. He had grown up in an urban environment in the Midwest, without a real father, and in a Pentecostal house church. But somehow during those breakfasts we had connected—really connected—as we slowly trusted each other with more and more of our lives.

There were a lot of "Oh, you too?" moments, to be sure. These were times when we realized how amazingly similar we were in our dreams, in our struggles, in our fears and in our hidden places of shame. But much of our connection came simply from the fact that we were taking the risk to trust ourselves to God and to one another as fully as we knew how. We had entered a room of grace with one another where no subject was off limits and where we each experienced the gift of simply being accepted and loved.

The intimacy we shared in that restaurant every Thursday eventually included my hearing bits and pieces of the deepest pain of Alex's life. Some mornings a little sliver would tumble out. Other times, it was obviously too embarrassing for him to talk about the depth of this crisis of faith and how it had exploded his entire social, vocational and theological world. On a couple of rare occasions he had taken me into the darkest corners, when we not only talked about the loss of their two babies but some of the emerging struggle around the word *father.* At that point, Alex had no relationship with his real father, and not much with his stepfather. And fatherhood had eluded him twice. Through the pain, even God's Fatherhood was clouded in mists of fear.

I could never have said that I understood the depth of Alex's pain. I didn't—and couldn't. But at least God had given me the gift of being able to be one of Alex's friends. There is no greater gift than to be able to stand by those you have come to love.

But I thought the dark days were over and that the thick fog of anger, pain, doubt and despair, which had so long obscured the Light in the center of Alex's life, was dissipating. And now this phone call. Was it happening yet again? What could I say? What would I encounter once I got to the hospital to join my brother in this latest vigil?

In the pages that follow, Alex (joined by his amazing wife, Jackie, in one chapter) tells the real story of the days that led up to Thanksgiving of 1996. This is not a story for people who like easy answers or quick fixes. But I can testify to the fact that it is a true story. It is the story of a "man of God" who almost ceased to be one—and whose life was changed forever by the God whom he nearly abandoned. And it is a story still being written.

Stephen A. Hayner

PREFACE

I wrote this book for the encouragement of good-hearted, well-intentioned, God-fearing believers who suddenly find themselves in the middle of crisis and turmoil. Many of these are people who continue to preach sermons, teach Sunday-school classes, train deacons, direct choirs, disciple new believers and lead small groups, yet their hearts have been broken and their dreams dashed.

They read Scripture that they are no longer inspired by, and they sing words to songs they no longer believe. They are merely going through the motions, partly because they are so loyal, partly because they are so numb.

Unfortunately, I know this from personal experience.

I am in my early forties and have been a Christian since age eleven and actively involved in ministry since I was a teenager. In my early teens I started leading my friends to the Lord. I have given over a thousand sermons, preached to crowds of tens of thousands, received numerous awards, pioneered a community development ministry and even started a few companies. Yet, none of these accolades mattered to me when my world began to fall apart.

I want to offer a message of hope to those who feel that God just sat there doing nothing while all hell broke loose in their lives. At the same time, I know there are no easy answers to these complex issues. I resented it when people offered simple solutions to me. Instead, I want you to know that I am with you on this very painful journey.

Take heart, trusting again after pain and loss is easier said than done. However, your sanity, joy and relationship with the Father are worth it.

SECTION ONE

ABANDONED

BY GOD

1

DIALING 911

Dialing 911 from my bedroom phone at 2:30 a.m.

"Emergency operator, may I help you?"

"Yes, my name is Alex Gee, my wife is nineteen weeks pregnant, and I think her water just broke! This is her second pregnancy, and," I paused, "we lost our first baby just like this."

"Someone will be right there, sir—what color is the fluid? Have you noticed any bleeding?"

"No, no, just a clear fluid." I turned from the phone. "Stay calm, just a second, Jackie. I'm trying to get help. . . . I'm sure the baby is just fine—but you have to stay calm."

"Sir? Hello? Sir? Try to stay calm. . . . Who is your wife's OB/GYN?"

"It's Dr. Koller! Uh—my wife is losing more fluid—hurry!" *Oh God, this isn't happening again—I can't do this again. . . . I can't handle another loss like this. . . . Let this be a dream—please let this be a dream!*

"We're coming, sir. The ambulance team should be there in just a moment."

Click.

I began to pray desperately, "Father, you promised that whatever I claim in your name will be done for me. I pray right now with authority, and I declare that my seed will be spared this time. Father, your Word says that the thief comes not but to steal, kill and destroy, but you have come to give us life and that more abundantly. I rebuke Satan, who has orchestrated this attack against my family and my faith. He is a liar, and I decree in Jesus' name that no weapon formed against me will prosper. You, O Lord, delight in the prosperity of your servant. You said that you would grant me the desires of my heart; all you have to do is speak one simple word and my baby will live. Please . . . please . . . please. In your name . . ."

I am haunted by crystal-clear memories of the events of that cruel night. My stomach did somersaults as loud sirens and red flashing lights notified my sleeping neighborhood that my unborn baby and my faith were again in need of resuscitation. In my mind's eye, I can still see the paramedics cautiously walking Jackie to the ambulance as vital amniotic fluid spills from her body. That snapshot let me know that we'd experience death again. All the while, saddened neighbors, who knew how much this baby meant to us, poured out onto their porches as an act of solidarity, offering up prayers and kind thoughts on my family's behalf as the ambulance whisked us away to St. Mary's Hospital.

Although the hospital was only four miles from our home, the ride felt like forever. I wasn't sure if I could remain hopeful, because things looked pretty bad again. I had never been that scared in my entire life. I actually shook myself twice on the way to the hospital because I couldn't tell if I were dreaming or not.

Hold on! But I'm one of the good ones—I thought I was special to God! This shouldn't be happening to me, right? It's not supposed to be like this, is it?

A MINISTER'S CRISIS OF FAITH

I knew how to be strong for other people in situations like this. I had dedicated myself to God as a young boy, started preaching at fifteen, got ordained at twenty and was already serving as a senior pastor when these events took place. It's funny how the rules seem to change when it's your own family and your own faith on the line.

The resident finished examining Jackie, and things didn't look good. They checked us into a room anyhow and told us that they were going to monitor Jackie and the baby. Within a few short hours Jackie spiked a terrible fever, which meant that she had developed an infection. Now there would be no more pleading with the doctors or God. The threat of infection meant inducing labor so as to save Jackie's life and perhaps her uterus.

This was our second pregnancy and our second trip to this same emergency room. We would be robbed of the joys of parenthood once again. It felt like a nightmare, too painful and too eerie to be real. I felt haunted, pursued even, by an evil force that was mocking my faith in God. I had what felt like an out-of-body experience—as though I could've chosen to float away to some safe, numb state of being. I never knew that mental breakdown could be so close.

The experience of loss was blurred by mental replays of our first loss: Victoria, only fourteen months prior. The same symptoms . . . the same on-duty nurse . . . the same sick feeling in the pit of my stomach . . . the same numbness. Now we were in a slow-motion replay of the worst day of my entire life. I didn't know what was worse—the unbearable pain that I was currently experiencing or the cruel, venomous flood of my unresolved hurt, anger and pain over the loss of Victoria. The strong forces of old and new grief tore my soul into pieces. At this point I was too numb to pick up those pieces and too distrustful of God to ask for his assistance.

Soon Jackie would once again deliver a daughter who would be too small to live more than just a few hours. And within the span of a single hour—sixty minutes—I would once again hold, name, footprint and say goodbye to a precious life that I helped to create. How many pastors dedicate and eulogize their own child on the same day? I did both that day with Alexis, just as I had with Victoria only a year before.

When Jackie and I lost Victoria, we were heartbroken. When we lost Alexis the very same way in the very next year, we were devastated. Furthermore, we experienced tremendous emotional pain and guilt that somehow we had failed God, who, in return, had chosen to reject or ignore our years of faithful Christian service. My underdeveloped theology had included the assumption that no bad thing would happen to God's faithful children and that God would grant anything they desired if they were just good enough.

Shaking Our Fists at God

I was extremely angry with God and didn't know how to deal with that. I thought that if I expressed my anger at him, he would destroy me—and yet I knew that if I didn't express myself to God, hurt and anger would destroy me.

Who teaches us how to properly shake our angry fists at God? Who dares?

When we have great anger, misunderstanding and pain festering inside, it is next to impossible to worship God, let alone pray. After finally concluding that God could not be any more distant from me than he already was and that I had absolutely nothing to lose, I threw caution to the wind and began to vent to the Father. I developed what I call a bad case of "spiritual Tourette's syndrome"—I shook my fist and blurted out whatever popped into my mind to God.

"You're not fair! I don't deserve this." *No response.*

"You must have an awfully short memory. I am one of the good ones." *No response.*

"Didn't it matter to you that I committed myself to chastity, sobriety and godly living beginning when I was a child—didn't that count for something?" *No response.*

"I have preached that Satan doesn't have the upper hand—that you are the Almighty One. Yet you allowed him to do this to me—twice! Are you who you say you are? Are you really all-powerful? Who's really calling the shots around here, you or Satan?" *No response.*

"You allow babies to have babies and then toss them in garbage containers, yet you keep letting this happen to us!" *No response.*

"What's so hard about giving two good people a baby, God? Haven't I given you the best years of my young life? Haven't I been true to you? Why weren't you there for us when we needed you the most? We don't ask you for much." *No response.*

"God, I had tremendous faith in you. You promised that if I ask anything in your name you will grant it. I have quoted your promises in Scripture back to you—why doesn't this work for me? I did what you told me to do; why didn't you do your part?" *Still no response.*

THE FUNERAL

My sense of abandonment was never stronger than when I sat in a funeral service for my second daughter, Alexis. That day I had written in my journal:

> *The funeral is today and I am stuck. If I don't attend, I'll never be able to live with myself. If I do attend, I'll never be able to forget certain images like the infant casket that looked an awful lot like a tiny white shoebox.*

I can remember the date, because it was my sister's first wedding anniversary. I was saddened that she had to spend her anniversary at a cemetery, and I was upset that her anniversary would always remind me of this day.

The sky is perfect and blue. Once again, nature seems to betray me—looking and acting like any other gorgeous day, but it isn't.

I stood in line at the flower shop with miniature pink-and-white sweetheart roses in my hand. It looked like I was on my way to a baby dedication or a birthday party for a special little girl. Instead, I was on my way to my own daughter's memorial service. Everyone else in the shop wore happy smiles as they bought plants, bouquets and helium-filled balloons for loved ones. I wore dark sunglasses so that the sadness in my eyes wouldn't betray my torment. I prayed no one would ask where I was going with the pretty flowers.

Parents aren't supposed to buy flowers for their children's funerals. Parents are supposed to die first. Nothing about this hellish ordeal seemed right or fair to me.

What makes this memory particularly sad for me is that no one outside of my immediate family (mother, sister, stepfather and, of course, Jackie) knew that the ceremony was taking place. I couldn't bring myself to tell anyone, much less invite anyone. To do so would have been to admit that this was really happening.

In fact, Jackie did not attend. She said she simply could not do it.

I understood. I didn't want to either. I suppose that if I hadn't attended, I would've convinced myself that the entire ordeal was merely a horrible nightmare and I would eventually awake from this sleep.

Things went from bad to worse for me at the memorial service. As a pastor, I am used to the pomp and circumstance of funerals, which in my African American church tradition are called "homegoings," and they are huge celebrations.

There was no pomp today.
There were no pallbearers.
There was no pastor.

There was no joy.

No kind words expressed.

No one to say, "Ashes to ashes, dust to dust."

No one to say, "We've gone as far as we can go. . . . You're dismissed.

. . . Go in peace,

please return to your cars and drive safely."

And what would the minister have said to comfort us anyway? "Be of good cheer—she is with the Lord right now"? Or I love this one: "God must've needed her more than us."

What would the minister have said about her? "She lived a good, long healthy life"? Would he have talked about her hobbies? Her classmates? Her work in the church? Her favorite songs? Favorite cartoons? Favorite toy? Favorite teacher?

No, because no one knew these things. No one gave us the time and opportunity to discover these things. And I felt like a failure because I couldn't even speak on her behalf other than to say that her mother and I created her in love. In hindsight, I am glad there was no minister. I would have hated him or her for even attempting to be on God's side by saying something "spiritual."

My mother, my sister, my stepfather just sat there with me. We tried to make small talk about heaven and seeing the baby again. It didn't work for me. The thought of heaven and God didn't particularly warm my heart. I suppose that my attitude wouldn't have been very welcome in heaven anyway.

But what kind of homegoing was this?

What do you do when you're experiencing the worst days of your life and God still refuses to make an appearance?

2

ARE YOU THERE, GOD?

My tears have been my food
day and night,
while men say to me all day long,
"Where is your God?"

PSALM 42:3

God's ways rarely make sense to us. The book of Isaiah says, "My thoughts are not your thoughts, neither are your ways my ways" (55:8). And when God's ways don't make sense to us, the result is a feeling of utter neglect and abandonment.

Dr. Susan Davidson, a wonderful perinatologist, came into Jackie's hospital room and gave her an ultrasound. Our baby was vibrant, swimming and flipping around like an Olympic synchronized swimmer. I breathed a sigh of relief, thinking everything was OK—the baby looked completely healthy.

She was. For her in-utero world.

At nineteen weeks, she was not healthy enough for the harsh realities of my world.

Dr. Davidson ordered a bunch of equipment and prepared for emergency delivery because Jackie had lost so much embryonic fluid.

"Dr. Davidson," I asked, "where is the neonatal equipment?"

The look on her face was incredulous—she hadn't realized that until that moment I was not aware that my daughter would not live.

It was the first and only time I had ever seen a doctor cry.

She delivered my firstborn child. And to our surprise, although she was very small and premature, my daughter was born alive, which meant we needed to footprint her and name her.

We called her Victoria and held her until she slipped out of our arms into eternity.

Personal Abandonment

From an early age, I was taught that God could do anything—but fail. My Sunday school teachers and mentors portrayed the Father as a God who could never ever make mistakes.

Holding my newly-born-but-quickly-dying daughter in the delivery room of St. Mary's Hospital that dark morning, I begged to differ. My teachers were wrong—because I had been wronged. God failed me—miserably!

Perhaps God was not as powerful as we had been led to believe.

That ill-fated morning, I lost a daughter, a Father and my faith. What was I to do with all of the "fables" I had been taught about this great God who would rescue those in need? Tales of how he parted seas, split rocks, fed the masses, healed diseases, raised the dead. Scripture seemed like much ado over nothing!

I was aware of what God could do for me, but I was not yet in a place to understand what he was trying to do within me.

I was unable to realize that hardship that builds character is as much the work of God as are his great public exploits. I couldn't grasp the concept of God working beneath the surface within the landscape of our souls. So I wasn't able to comprehend God when he was merely changing my attitude, molding my heart, reordering my priorities and shaping my character

What's the point of all the inspiring stories of the Bible if they don't apply to us? I had preached these stories for years. I had believed them for even longer. I had told these stories to terminally ill patients in hospitals. I had encouraged recovering drug addicts with these stories. I had led people to Christ with these stories. . . . And my faith was aborted because of these stories.

Jackie and I were kind, giving people who wanted a baby more than anything else in the world. To be quite honest, I had been looking forward to this baby's arrival for a long time. I had been planning and preparing to become a dad since I was a child.

So when the dark night of my soul fell, I had no candle or flashlight to guide me. The terrain was unfamiliar to me, so I couldn't feel my way around either. I did what I had been taught to do when I was in a bind: I cried out to God. I was certain that God would answer me the way he answered David: "This poor man called, and the LORD heard him" (Psalm 34:6).

I expected God to do what I saw him do in the Bible: rescue me! But he didn't come. Not the way I wanted him to. And when it became apparent that God was not going to come rescue me, I began to lose it; faith didn't work for me. For me, an out-of-sight God was an AWOL God.

I lost faith that God existed the way I had thought he did.

I lost faith that I could move God instantly.

I lost faith that I mattered to God.

I lost the innocence of my childlike faith, which perhaps was really adult naiveté disguised as childlike faith.

I felt what my friend Ken Gire expressed in his book *Windows of the Soul:* "I don't know who I am fighting, God or the devil. All I know is that someone won today, and it wasn't me." He felt defeated and abandoned.

So when I felt my prayers bounced off the walls of the hospital delivery room, I felt soulless. Invisible. Insignificant. Duped. Cursed. And it soon became apparent that I had to either wait for God to come to me and lead me out of that darkness or risk stumbling and really hurting myself—or someone else. This is where I began to lose it; my faith wasn't working for me.

The anger, disappointment and disillusionment felt unbearable. My broken heart was forced to wrestle with wrenching questions: Who is God? Who am I? Don't we have a relationship? Didn't we have an agreement—*I'll be good if you will*—God?

As a kid, I used to hear other kids say things like "My dad can whip your dad!" Or kids would threaten to tell their dads on playground bullies. I never boasted in these ways, because my father and stepfather were emotionally distant men. As far as I was concerned, neither of them was a fighter, nor did they have any interest in protecting me.

As a believer, however, I have often boasted in prayer, Scripture and preaching that Jehovah God could whip all other gods. But when the fighter's bell rang at St. Mary's Hospital, signifying that the first round had begun, my heavenly Father didn't seem to be much of a fighter either and threw in the towel.

BLAMING MY FATHER

Feeling abandoned by my heavenly Father reminded me of some hidden personal abandonment that I'd long forgotten. When I was one year old, my mother decided to leave her physically abusive husband so as to protect my innocence. My mother left so that I wouldn't grow up to despise my abusive father the way my father grew up to despise his abusive father. My mother left so that I would not be hurt. From then on my father stayed away (for the most part) because *he* was very hurt by the loss of his family.

I did occasionally see my father over the years, because Mom made a point of my knowing my father's side of the family. These meetings were sporadic, and I often felt like an outsider around my own extended family. To add insult to injury, my mother remarried years later, and I felt even more out of place around my extended stepfamily. Although my stepfather was kind to me, he was emotionally distant, and his limited education rendered him insecure around me. This usually led to a practice known as "dumbing down"—I downplayed my abilities so as to not intimidate, and thereby alienate, my stepfather. I wanted a father's attention so badly that I pretended to be someone I wasn't with my stepfather in order to secure his affection.

I don't understand all of the psychological ins and outs. I do know that because of my experiences with my earthly fathers, I have a haunting fear that people will pull away from me if I don't live up to their expectations or meet their needs.

I hoped that my childhood decision to work hard, be liked and be successful would help to smother my fear of abandonment. In actuality, my fears smoldered underneath the surface of my busyness. I learned to manage my emotions at a very young age. Perhaps this kept me safe. Perhaps it kept me sane.

I unconsciously kept tabs on all of my failures and weaknesses, whether in grades or social awkwardness or delayed athletic development or even my struggle with puberty (or its struggle with me). I somehow thought that I would have had the confidence required for adolescence and middle school if I'd had a father in my life. It was easy to blame my dad for everything—he wasn't there.

From a very young age, I knew what I wanted to be when I grew up: the president of the United States, a teacher, a businessman and a dad. Other boys talked about wanting to be football players or cowboys when they grew up. I don't remember any of my friends stating an ambition of being a dad. I can't explain it, but one of the things I was certain I was destined to become as an adult was a father.

When I grew up and got married, I assumed that hope would be fulfilled. I realized that a man gets two shots at fatherhood: having one and being one. I could never go back in time and have a father; however, I could become one. So I thought.

During the first years of marriage, busyness with work and ministry helped me forget how much pain and hopelessness I had always lived with—until I experienced the loss of my daughters. Where was God then? The Lord could have helped me make sense of my entire life. He could have redeemed all the unpleasant things of my life by simply allowing me to become a father. So I thought.

With the losses of Victoria and Alexis, my heart was broken into tiny pieces. I began to wonder if God was capable of abandonment just like my earthly dad. God had not only chosen to ignore my childhood pain, he had failed to rectify his neglect by making me a dad, even though I begged him for a child like a man pleading for his life.

In a way, I *was* pleading for my life—and my faith. My need for a father and my need to become a father had somehow become entwined with my understanding of my heavenly Father's responsibility to me. My wounds hijacked my faith and faithfulness. My perspective of God and his commitment to me was obscured.

I was drowning in self-absorption. I was too blind to save myself and too disoriented to articulate what I truly needed. Someone was going to have to rescue me, because I was in no place to help myself.

3

CHILDREN ARE A
GIFT FROM THE LORD

Children are a gift from the LORD;

they are a reward from him.

PSALM 127:3 NLT

H as it been five minutes yet? Please go in the bathroom and look for me, Alex; I am too nervous!"

Jackie and I were complete novices when it came to home pregnancy devices—we'd never used them before.

"Omigosh! I see a plus sign—Jackie, it's positive!"

Jackie yelled and jumped up and down, and I cried. This was one of the happiest moments in our life. With four years of marriage experience under our belt, we were so excited and so ready for the next frontier—parenting.

All sorts of wonderful thoughts flooded our heads and hearts: *Who do we tell first? How do we tell them? Do we want to know the sex of the baby? What kind of parents will we be? When is the baby due?*

Although we hadn't put pressure on ourselves to begin our family too soon, both Jackie and I looked forward to parenting. We had a good relationship and a healthy walk with the Lord. God had always been at the center of our relationship. At this point, a baby felt like sweet icing on an already wonderful cake. I was a bivocational pastor and worked at the university as an academic adviser; Jackie also worked there as a policy analyst. We were grateful that we both had college degrees and stable finances, which took some fear out of the prospect of parenting. We were confident that we could provide a safe, loving environment for our new baby. In fact, we started a college fund for our future children three years before we decided to begin our family.

Apparently, none of this seemed to matter to the Lord.

It didn't matter that we were good people.

It didn't matter that we had remained sexually pure until our wedding night.

It didn't matter that we were leading an exciting church ministry.

It didn't matter that we had begun looking at nursery furnishings.

It didn't matter that we were so ready for this baby.

Before we could register for a single Lamaze class, before an invitation could be mailed for a baby shower, before we could become used to the idea of becoming parents, our greatest dream became our worst nightmare, just a week and a half after Mother's Day.

POST MOTHER'S DAY

Jackie had been feeling fine. She was glowing from all the excitement of being pregnant on Mother's Day. I still have a snapshot of her in the maternity dress that she got especially for this holiday. I had never seen her happier.

The following week was a bit intense. One day Jackie said that she felt a strange sensation in her cervix, but everyone assumed it was normal baby pains. She tried to relax, but I could see stress in her face. She went to bed early that night as I stayed home to entertain a friend who was celebrating his birthday. The evening was cut short when Jackie called me upstairs to tell me that she thought she was leaking some fluid. We called an on-call nurse from our clinic and were told to get Jackie to the hospital as soon as possible.

With the sickest feeling in the pit of my stomach, I tried to make small talk with my horrified wife in order to keep her calm. But although I am a motivational speaker and the quintessential encourager, I felt as if my words were bouncing off the walls of our bedroom. Poor Jackie looked dazed as she hurried to dress herself. She wanted to scream and cry but was afraid that giving in to her emotions would somehow make her worst nightmare come true.

I never pictured myself as one who would call in a favor with God. Still, having served him since my childhood, I was confident that he would turn this ugly situation around for his glory—and my faithfulness. I had never prayed so hard. It seemed to me at the time that the Lord must have a very short memory. Or maybe he doesn't like to have favors called in. Whatever the case, I didn't hear back from him that night. He was just as silent as Jackie—but I knew why *she* was keeping quiet.

If children are a gift from the Lord, what was this—a reprimand? a wake-up call? punishment? It certainly was no gift! What kind of God would give my wife a precious life in her womb, just to rob her—us—like this? This is the kind of pain that makes believers question the sovereignty of God. What kind of God would allow this to happen to his faithful followers?

As if it hadn't been bad enough to go through this horrible ordeal, we would experience the same hell again in just a year with the loss of our second child, Alexis.

4

A Message from Jackie Gee

Who can find a virtuous and capable wife?
She is worth more than precious rubies. . . .
Her children stand and bless her.
Her husband praises her.

PROVERBS 31:10, 28 NLT

Alex and I are certainly different people. He is extremely extroverted and therefore prefers to process his painful experiences verbally with others. I, on the other hand, prefer to mull over issues in the privacy and solitude of my own soul. So I would never write a book that tells the world of my fears, failures and battles with faith. This is not to say that I haven't struggled with each of these.

When we experienced those dark nights of our souls, we struggled to find helpful resources to guide us through our pain. There were books on miscarriage, but we found very little on the loss of premature babies. Furthermore, we found even fewer materials that helped us express our profound anger and disappointment with our God. So I do think this book is needed.

At the same time I must admit that a part of me hates that this story is in print. Alex's vivid memory and vulnerable approach to the subject makes me realize that the pain is not as far away as I'd like to believe. And although my pain is obviously still there, I understand that it is much different from Alex's.

My pain was fear—fear that I had somehow failed Alex as a wife. I knew how important family was to him. He grew up in a family where children were valued and appreciated. They went on family vacations. They had family home movies—*and they watched them!* His mother attended his track meets, parent-teacher meetings and award ceremonies. I knew that he had so much that he wanted to give to his children someday. I wasn't going to let anything keep that from happening. Not finances. Not fear. Not career. Not even ministry.

Some things are beyond one's own control, unfortunately.

Losing Victoria

One thing Alex hasn't mentioned is that before we lost our first baby, Victoria, at seventeen weeks, I almost had a miscarriage with her at ten weeks. I worked in the tallest building on the University of Wisconsin-Madison campus, and my office was on the eighteenth floor. One day as I stood up to reach for something in my office, I noticed that my chair was full of blood. There was no cramping or warning, just profuse bleeding. Words cannot begin to express my horror. I collapsed and fell on the floor but managed to call for my assistant, who called the ambulance. The paramedics had to bring the stretcher all the way to the top of our building to get me. That was the worst day of my life up to that point. And although the emergency-room doctors would eventually run tests, check me out and give me a clean bill of health, the *real* worst day of my life would occur in just a few months.

Once again, I was back in the emergency room because of losing a lot of fluid. Back in those days the doctors didn't try any heroics. I was immediately given medicines that cause contractions and delivery. Because I delivered so early, I didn't have the benefit of Lamaze classes, so I didn't know what to expect or how to deal with the painful contractions. There were no nurses to coach me; Dr. Davidson was flanked by Alex and his mother—two unlikely midwives. Within a few hours, I delivered a very, very small baby.

Our hospital was incredibly sensitive to grieving families. The staff gave us baby clothing knitted by volunteers so that we could dress Victoria. The nurses took pictures of us holding the baby. She lived for nearly an hour. It was probably the sweetest—*and shortest*—forty-five minutes of my life. The doctor who delivered Victoria diagnosed that I have what is known as an incompetent cervix. My cervix cannot shut completely during pregnancy, and the weight of the baby forces the cervix open, causing premature birth.

MY FEAR AND INSECURITY

My response was fear. I feared that I was the only person in the world who could make Alex's dream of becoming a dad (and whole) a reality. And I couldn't do that. I never knew the voices of doubt and accusation could be so convincing—and loud. Insecurities about being good enough to be Alex's wife surfaced. Concern about being strong enough to be a pastor's wife surfaced. Would Alex blame me more than I blamed myself? And though he would never say anything so cruel to me, would he secretly feel these things for the rest of our lives? I wondered if God was punishing me like he punished the barren women in the Old Testament. What did I do to deserve punishment? And how could I make amends for it?

I had always been a fairly strong person. I excelled in academics as well as collegiate track and field. I was accustomed to making things happen. With a national Junior Olympics championship in the women's 400 meters in high school; a second-place finish in the Big Ten Indoor Conference meet in the 400 meters as a college sophomore; and a University of Wisconsin-Madison school relay record (Alex tells me that it still stands today), I had never just stood around and hoped things would happen. I *helped* things to happen. But now I began to wonder if all the years of training, weightlifting and competing had somehow caused my tiny body to not be able to carry a child. I couldn't bear the thought of that.

Maybe the hardest thing for me in all of this was watching Alex's interaction with little children in our church and community. His sister, Lilada, invited us to be in the birthing room when her daughter, Alexandra, was born. She wanted us to experience the miracle of childbirth since we would most likely never have this experience personally. Alex would make frequent trips to the opposite side of town just to hold his beautiful little niece. He said that he felt like God was massaging his aching heart when he held Alexandra.

It's interesting, people ooh and ah when they see men playing with little babies. But if you are a woman who cannot have babies or who has lost or miscarried children, when you hold a child you feel all the eyes of pity that stare at you. (Only a woman who has been here knows the truth of which I speak.) I don't know if people think we're going to run off with the baby or become so uncontrollably emotional that we'll upset the child we're holding, or what! I just know that I hated being pitied just as much as I hated the pain. In fact, the pity meant shame for me, and that was excruciatingly painful. Maybe I've watched too many soap operas, but I didn't want to spend the rest of my life staring at children and their parents in playgrounds wondering what it would've been like for me. I just wanted out of this slump.

PREGNANT AGAIN

My game plan (remember, I am a competitor) was to get pregnant again as soon as possible. I thought that if I could be pregnant a second time before the due date of my first baby, the memory of the loss wouldn't be so unbearable. So I monitored ovulation cycles and tried my darnedest to get pregnant quickly. Life became very complicated with timing cycles and ovulation, buying home pregnancy tests, reading results and doing all of this over and over again month after month. Getting pregnant was like having a part-time job. Although I didn't become pregnant by Victoria's due date, I did become pregnant a second time a few months thereafter with Alexis.

We were very cautious with this second pregnancy. Alex and I decided that I wouldn't attend his family reunion in Jackson, Mississippi, because he didn't want me to travel that far by car while pregnant. My OB/GYN put a cerclage (a securing stitch) in my cervix to keep it securely shut during my pregnancy and avoid another heartbreaking loss. We held our breath for the first seventeen weeks of pregnancy because that was the point at which we lost Victoria. Week eighteen felt like a marathoner's finish line. Alex was so excited and I was so relieved. To my dismay, at nineteen weeks I began to feel some familiar discomfort in my cervix while in the office one day. I tried to calm my heart by assuring myself that lightning would not—could not—strike twice in the same place.

Alex rushed me to the hospital, and because I was considered high risk, I was able to see a doctor right away. Everything checked out fine, and I was released the same day. But I knew something wasn't right although everything looked normal to the medical staff.

Within two days I would be admitted to the hospital and lose my second daughter, Alexis, to premature birth. Although the doctors still aren't 100 percent sure of the cause, they suspect that bacteria grew in my cerclage and caused my water membranes to rupture. The cerclage that was supposed to save my baby became the culprit for her demise. How ironic.

NEEDING GOD

Lightning did strike twice in the same place—in my soul. It struck all the parched areas and set them aflame. Guilt, fear, failure, worthlessness, cursedness and judgment burned my heart. The despair was so intense that I felt possessed by gloom. The shame was so heavy that I found it difficult to look my own friends and family in the eye for fear that my own eyes would betray the fragility and hopelessness of my heart.

Alex blamed God for much of his pain. I knew that if we were going to come out of this with any shred of sanity or faith, God himself would have to rescue us. We were in way too deep for any human being to reach us.

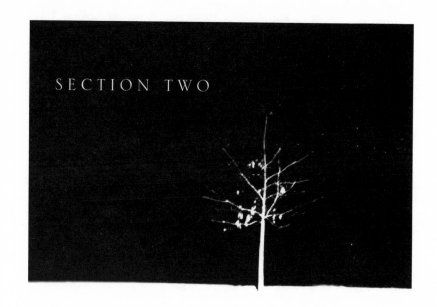

SECTION TWO

WHO IS GOD

REALLY?

5

A Moment of Truth

After we lost Victoria, I couldn't wrap my mind or my theology around the fact that my Father would allow my heart to be broken in so many little pieces. My pain challenged everything I thought I knew about God: his grace, his power, his sovereignty, his love, his care. Where was God? And how could he be so far removed from my cry?

The pain in my heart was so intense, so dense, it almost destroyed me. I couldn't attend church—and I was the senior pastor. I couldn't pray. I couldn't read Scripture. All I could do was sleep, because it was my only escape from the torment of reality.

Early one Wednesday morning I lay immobilized in bed, just staring at the ceiling. I remember that it was a Wednesday because my mother had invited me to the weekly Wednesday-morning prayer meeting so that friends could pray for Jackie and me. I declined the invitation because I couldn't muster the emotional energy to get out of bed and face a roomful of people who wanted to say something deep and profound to me:

- "Maybe God has something so special for you and Jackie to do that a child would've hindered his plan."

- "At least you'll see the baby in heaven."
- "Maybe God wants you to adopt."
- "God knows what's best."
- "We'll pray harder next time."

How could I attend an intimate prayer gathering and utter sincere prayers to a God who would allow me to suffer like this? What would I say to him? What would he say to me?

We had nothing to say to each other, I deduced, so I stayed in bed—boycotting a weekly prayer meeting that I had organized.

At about 8:30 a.m., the strangest thing occurred. A wave of peace pulsated through my heart. This presence was so strong that it shocked me. Having grown up in a worship tradition in which people expect to experience the presence of God, I was very familiar with this sensation. It was the presence of the Holy Spirit.

Quickly turning over and looking at the clock, I realized that the prayer meeting had just begun.

People were praying for me! Friends were lifting my family and me to the Lord. I was touched! I was comforted. I was surprised!

Then I was horrified. *Oh noooooooooooooooo!*

If I was right, and this was the touch of the Spirit, I was in big trouble! Why would the Holy Spirit be so near me? I hadn't prayed in weeks. I hadn't read Scripture in weeks.

How could God be so near if I hadn't invited him?

I had blamed God for every bit of pain that I was enduring. And although I did not have all the answers to my many questions, I did know this: if God was comforting me, he could not also be the one who was tormenting me! I was certain that God is unpredictable; however, I was even more certain that he could not torment and tame simultaneously.

I had been blaming the wrong one for my pain. God was my Advocate. My Redeemer. My Comforter. Yet I had made him my Scapegoat—the one I blamed for all my troubles.

Because someone had to be blamed . . .

I was still very far from understanding the full picture of this dark night of my soul. However, I experienced a tremendous breakthrough that Wednesday morning. God was not my enemy, nor was he angry with me. God's nature doesn't allow him to be good *and* evil. Although I still don't understand why God chose to allow me to experience the tremendous hardship of losing two daughters, I know now that he is never the author of evil.

RECOGNIZING JESUS

I found myself in the story of the two disciples who meet Jesus on the Emmaus Road (Luke 24) after the crucifixion. They do not recognize the Savior! Yet the disciple Cleopas spoke with honesty to the "stranger" he did not recognize about his frustation with the way Jesus had handled things. His honesty freed me to begin venting my anger with God as well. This newfound honesty with God brought a new depth to my relationship with him.

In Luke 24, Jesus takes Cleopas and the other disciple back to the Law and Prophets because they had obviously gotten far away from the truth. Jesus uses Scripture to remind these disciples of God's true nature and his plan for redemption. The nature of God is to pursue those he loves. God's plan was that Jesus needed to die, not conquer Rome and end Roman occupation at that time. So Jesus adjusts the perspective of his followers and gives them a reality check. He shows them that what they think they understand about the Almighty is very far from the truth, and he gives them a new view.

Like them, I saw a new side of God that Wednesday morning.

6

IS THIS GOD'S WRATH?

Then he took the cloak that had fallen from
him and struck the water with it.
"Where now is the LORD, the God of Elijah?"

2 KINGS 2:14

Elisha asked the question that many of us want the answer to—
where is God?

I am sure Elisha was feeling very sad that Elijah had gone to
heaven. He didn't feel prepared to handle the mantle that had just
been dropped on him, and his mentor had suddenly disappeared.

What would be the sign that God was truly present with him?
"When he struck the water, it divided to the right and to the left, and
he crossed over" (2 Kings 2:14). That was a clear sign.

There always seemed to be clear signs for people in the Bible. They
heard God's voice; they wrestled with angels; they baked cakes for
heavenly beings; they walked through waters on dry land; they saw

the sun stand still; they witnessed the hand of God in miraculous ways.

But what about the times when the signs aren't clear? It would be so much easier to be obedient to God if we could just have a sign that he cares for us. Without signs, we may start to wonder: *Has God abandoned me? Is God mad at me?*

EXPERIENCING GOD'S DISCIPLINE

We often confuse wrath and discipline.

Discipline is what God does when you and I do what we've been instructed not to do. Discipline can also be a form of instruction. Its motivation is love and compassion. We experience it when we are suffering due to choices we make involving lying, cheating, stealing and so on. We experience discipline when we elevate something else to the place of God in our lives.

The end result of discipline is that people are *restored* to the presence of God. The end result of wrath is that they are removed from the presence of God.

As you read the Old Testament, you witness recurring phenomena: The enemies of God are destroyed. The friends of God are disciplined, proved and chastised. However, they are never destroyed.

The Lord's plan was an interesting one. He would allow the punishment of his beloved children when they continued to disobey. But the purpose was never to ignore them, or abandon them, or demean them.

God constantly told his wayward children that if they didn't serve him in their own land, they would serve strange gods in a foreign land: "And when the people ask, 'Why has the LORD our God done all this to us?' you will tell them, 'As you have forsaken me and served foreign gods in your own land, so now you will serve foreigners in a land not your own'" (Jeremiah 5:19). However, when God's children learned their lesson—even temporarily—he would rescue them and treat them like royalty:

> This third I will bring into the fire;
> > I will refine them like silver
> > and test them like gold.
> They will call on my name
> > and I will answer them;
> I will say, "They are my people,"
> > and they will say, "The LORD is our God." (Zechariah 13:9)

So where is God when we're being disciplined for our actions? Right behind us.

When the Lord is getting on us in order to help rid our lives of destructive vices, it is out of love. "No discipline seems pleasant at the time, but painful. Later on, however, it produces a harvest of righteousness and peace for those who have been trained by it" (Hebrews 12:11).

When we feel the warmth of the Father's love on our backside, it is proof that he has not abandoned us. During times of chastisement, he is right behind us.

But sometimes his training is not discipline because we have done something wrong. My high school track coach purposefully designed our workouts to develop endurance, speed, focus and discipline. His plan was to make practice so hard that track meets would seem like fun. Most teams became tense at meets; we were relieved, therefore relaxed. Our city championship title was awarded in a fancy stadium before hundreds of cheering fans; however, our victory was earned on the small, laneless cinder track of our practice field.

I thought my coaches were out of touch with modern training methods. There were times that our team cursed them silently under our breath. We figured they were trying to live and win vicariously through us. We practiced coming out of the starting blocks; we practiced handoffs with batons, ran drills, lifted weights, and jogged for hours and hours and miles and miles. We were certain the coaches were out to get us until we stood on the championship stand to receive our trophy. Then I understood: my coaches weren't angry with the team; they knew what it would take to make us champions. Our training wasn't punishment for losing a competition—it was preparation for *winning* one.

WHAT IS GOD'S WRATH?

A few years after Jackie's and my second bereavement, I was starting to understand that it was not God who caused the untimely deaths of my daughters. I still struggled, however, with understanding why he would use such devastating events to teach me important life lessons. My spiritual muscles were sore, I was out of breath, I couldn't take any more training. I wasn't convinced that God wasn't sadistic (enjoying seeing me in pain). I didn't want to learn from my losses because it felt as though the lesson would justify the loss. I had expected more nurture and sympathy from God, not a take-home exam. God's desire to teach me a lesson from my pain felt like a master shoving a dog's nose into a mess it has just made in the living room. At times, I still felt far from experiencing the love, blessings and prosperity I had grown accustomed to. I often thought I must have been very bad to need such a drastic lesson in life and faith. I struggled with feeling like I was on the front side of God's wrath.

With time I found books that pointed me to places in Scripture recounting how God shaped character through hardship. I read testimonies of others who promised that there was life after suffering. And although I really didn't want to acknowledge it, I began to understand that discipline and wrath cannot be more different from each other, though they are often confused. Discipline transforms us from hard-to-mold cold clay into a supple mass that is worked into a beautiful masterpiece that reflects and honors the Potter. But the process of being made supple can feel a lot like wrath.

God's wrath was never portrayed so vividly as when darkness covered the Earth as his Son died on the cross. That day God took on himself the sins and sinfulness of us all. It was the darkest day in history. But three days later was the brightest day in history, because the resurrection of Jesus meant that the sacrificial offering of his life for our acceptance was acceptable to the Father.

God is not interested in pouring out wrath on those who love him. The resurrection of Jesus is the evidence of the Father's acceptance of all who would approach him through Jesus. To reject those who call on Jesus would mean that the Father rejects Jesus himself and his selfless sacrifice. So I am learning to not say that I am experiencing God's wrath or hatred when things don't go my way. God will never reject us. Wrath is reserved for the enemies of God, not his children.

God *will* reject our idolatry. God will reject our meaningless offerings. God will reject our empty ritualistic prayers. But God will never reject his own child who diligently seeks him.

I am learning that I don't have to wait for the other shoe to drop with God. He is not hunting me down like some annoyed gardener trying to swat a pesky mosquito. The Father is looking for ways to love me, not swat me. At times I've gotten him all wrong.

If my suffering is not caused by God's wrath, then why do I suffer?

MISFORTUNE HAPPENS TO THE BEST OF US

It's not wrath. It's not judgment. It's not a consequence of our own actions.

It's life—and life happens.

Godly parents lose a child in a car accident. Virtuous women lose their husbands to adulterous relationships. Prayerful ministry leaders lose parents to Alzheimer's cruel grip. Faithful young married couples struggle with infertility. A courageous peacekeeper is accidentally stabbed while breaking up a fight. An innocent girl is sexually molested by a relative. A trusting boy is violated by a trusted church leader. A godly businessman who is gifted, fair and philanthropic loses his company due to a legal technicality that is beyond his control. An accomplished musician discovers that physical damage caused by an automobile accident makes playing the piano excruciatingly painful.

On the flip side, sometimes it seems as though the wicked experience goodness without measure:

> You are always righteous, O LORD,
>> when I bring a case before you.
> Yet I would speak with you about your justice:
>> Why does the way of the wicked prosper?
>> Why do all the faithless live at ease? (Jeremiah 12:1)

Misfortune is very difficult to accept, because often there is no one to blame. Repercussions from our own actions are understandable, even if we don't agree that we should be responsible for our choices. Spiritual discipline, though very difficult, is a result of our own wrongdoings. This is not the case with misfortune. Misfortune has no rhyme or reason.

> As [Jesus] went along, he saw a man blind from birth. His disciples asked him, "Rabbi, who sinned, this man or his parents, that he was born blind?"
>
> "Neither this man nor his parents sinned," said Jesus, "but

this happened so that the work of God might be displayed in his life." (John 9:1-3)

It is hard to believe that something as drastic as blindness could just be a mishap. The disciples wanted accountability for this situation. Where does the buck stop? "It's no one's fault—this is a setup for the glory of God to be revealed" was the gist of Jesus' response.

I believe that this is one of those places where I began to unravel. I didn't see trouble coming.

There is no warning sign that a seemingly healthy pastor is diagnosed with cancer.

No one saw the drunk driver heading in the wrong direction down a one-way street.

A Christian family loses both of its young parents, both of whom are ministers, to untimely deaths resulting from illness.

A stray bullet takes out one of the community's most promising athletes.

A loving father comes home from work to find his teenage son dead from an apparent suicide.

A praying grandmother finds herself raising her grandchildren because her daughter is strung out on drugs.

The list goes on and on. The world is a wicked place. Sin, brokenness and destruction are all around.

I am not exempt from hardship just because of my faith in God. Understanding this sobering truth was the turning point for my healing.

WHERE IS GOD WHEN WE SUFFER MISFORTUNE?

Scripture tells us that God loves the downtrodden. The widows. The orphans. The children. The manic and depressed. The elderly. The outcast. The poor.

He is drawn to those whose lives seem to be over. And he gives them grace, mercy and his loving presence. Where is God when we suffer? Standing right beside us—so that we never have to know what it means to stand alone.

Many women have experienced a deep sense of loneliness when they have been abandoned by their husbands and left to care for small children. The strain is compounded for those who have never worked outside the home. One mom I know had a special-needs child with a deadly illness. After her husband left, this mother worked hard to care for her family and started a home-based business that became quite successful. She has been able to raise her children and pay the medical bills. God was with her.

Elisabeth Elliot, whose husband was killed when he tried to reach out to the Huaorani people of Ecuador, saw the hand of God in the midst of her pain. And she was able to love, forgive and minister to her husband's murderers.

God has used the pain of my own fatherlessness to propel me to mentor and disciple men who are plagued by similar father issues. I actually experience the Lord's healing as I reach out to help other men.

The Lord never misses an opportunity to show his solidarity with us in our pain. He is always there. We just need to have patience and watch for his presence.

7

THE RADICAL TRUTH
ABOUT GOD'S LOVE

Although God's methodology often seems strange to us, his love should never be.

God loves us more than words could ever express. In fact, Scripture tells us that God rejoices over us with singing. The Hebrew word for "singing" means to move about rhythmically. This means that when the Father thinks of us, it actually causes him to *move rhythmically.*

Can you imagine the Almighty dancing at the thought of us? The foxtrot? The Charleston? The waltz? The jitterbug? The samba? The bump? The twist? Salsa? The cabbage patch?

I now realize that I am far from being forsaken by God. It is not God's nature to forsake us. It is God's nature to love us, pursue us and protect us. Neglecting his followers is not an option for God.

Scripture is given to us to help us understand how God operates. Scripture is a snapshot of the Father's essence: his mercy, his love, his care, his pursuit of us. In fact, all of Scripture is about the Father's passionate pursuit of his wayward children.

GIVING GOD A BAD RAP

Unfortunately, I gave God a pretty bad rap as a practical joker. From my childhood I'd been taught to lean on God as my source, but during my crisis he seemed to stand back and do nothing. It felt like a friend offering a chair and then pulling it out as I sit down. I wondered, *Is God the solution or is he the cause of our problems?* And because it's not "spiritually correct" to question the Almighty, I locked these painful issues inside, and my presumptuous faith died a slow death of anger, cynicism and doubt.

But God is not a practical joker. He does not pose as a celestial vending machine, handing us a roll of coins just to display a sign saying, "Sorry! Out of order." Yet I have often seen him this way. How do I take my problems to God when I think he either created the problems or sat silent while my world fell apart? In order to change this view, I must understand who he really is and who he desires to be in my life.

Consider the irony of being a good single mother—especially a recently divorced single mother! She is the one who waits on her children hand and foot. She is the one who makes sure that they are up for school, dressed for school, prepared for school and picked up from school. Yet when the children feel anger and frustration about the absence of their father, it is often the mother who receives the brunt of this frustration because she's the one who's there—she hasn't left. This is terribly unfair, but it happens nonetheless. Like a grieving child, I blamed the One who is really loyal to me, our heavenly Father.

I seem to have been suckered into believing that my covenant with God would somehow make me popular, successful and likable. And in return I would be humbly appreciative and adoring.

Hah! He never fulfills his end of that bargain. And neither do I.

The true nature of God is actually better than a bottomless vending machine. A machine only can dispense stuff. God wants to dispense values, character, insights, dignity and love—attributes of God's character. The traits God wants to give us are forged in the fiery furnaces of life, experienced in the valleys of disappointment, inherited from the death of our dreams.

And just when God is about to impart these wonderful traits to my soul, I hoist the anchor and set sail in another direction because I figure that God just pulled a fast one. God's methodology almost never makes sense to me. This is why it is so important to understand God's nature.

REAL TRUST

Here's an excerpt from my personal journal, exploring what it means to trust.

> *I was up early this morning praying for friends and family . . . their families, their careers, their finances, their ministries and their dreams.*
>
> *I heard the Spirit ask me a question: "Do you trust me?"*
>
> *I almost spoke in haste to answer appropriately by saying, "Yes! Of course!"*
>
> *I heard a gentle voice reminding me, "Trust is not faith."*
>
> *Faith is built upon our understanding of God's ability and proven track record. It is believing that God can . . .*
>
> *Trust is different. It is built upon our understanding of God's nature. We may believe that God can (particularly for others), but often doubt that he will (particularly for us, personally).*
>
> *Your faith may tell you that God is able. However, your trust is telling you that God is partial (he favors some over others); God is a*

faultfinder; God is angry with you; God is secretly getting revenge on you; God is not fully loving or accepting of you; or simply, God is not interested in the things that interest you!

Faith is based upon your perspective of God's ability. Trust is built upon your perspective of God's nature (good vs. evil . . . loving vs. faultfinding).

Many sons/daughters of God are very faithful in the things of God but distrustful of the person of God. If we feel that we are unworthy of being loved freely, we tend to project that upon God and see him as an uncaring God. If we are afraid to live life fully by experiencing true liberty in being authentic, we tend to project that upon God and deduce that bondage is his will for us.

We must reconcile our faith and our trust if we are going to walk closely with the Lord.

If we receive blessings from God because we merely have faith, but don't experience intimacy with God, we are both robbing and fooling ourselves.

The Father longs to have us know him and his true nature. The Father longs to have us trust him.

WHAT GOD GIVES US

God offers us himself: His nature. His attributes. His heart. His patience. His humility.

These life-changing and godly attributes aren't the products of faith; rather, they are the products of faithfulness. These attributes don't come from being good—*they come from being battered.* So the hardships that we experience are not God's wrath. It is actually the love of God that allows us to suffer hardship so that we can become more sympathetic and trusting.

This is tremendously good news. God's nature will not allow him to taunt, tempt or traumatize humans. From the beginning of time, God has been trying to convey one true message to his children: "You are the objects of my affection!"

"For God so loved the world . . ." John 3:16 is one of the most loved and memorized verses of the entire Bible. I often quote this Scripture to the lost and unsaved; how wonderful it would be if we believers really believed this verse for ourselves! Believers preach that God is willing to save mass murderers, child molesters, false prophets, drug dealers and death row inmates, yet it's hard for us to believe that our heavenly Father has any mercy for his redeemed children who find themselves struggling with their faith or understanding Scripture.

"[The LORD] knows how we are formed, / he remembers that we are dust" (Psalm 103:14). In other words, he has not forgotten or ignored our humanity and sinful nature. Yet he loves us—very deeply. God's love for us is not based on our ability to do good deeds; God loves us because we have been created by him and for him. His love is not based on merit, flawlessness or human righteousness. This is what is meant by unconditional love.

"Before I formed you in the womb I knew you, / before you were born I set you apart; / I appointed you as a prophet to the nations" (Jeremiah 1:5). The Hebrew word for "knew" in this verse is *yada'*. This word means to perceive, to understand, to know through reflection and revelation. Jeremiah has been attempting to convince God that he is too young and inexperienced to fulfill the ministry to which he is being called. God is telling Jeremiah that he isn't moved by his credentials or résumé—or lack thereof. God tells Jeremiah that he knows all about him, good and bad; God understands him inside out; God has a revelation of him, both strengths and weaknesses.

With all this in mind, God still wants to use Jeremiah. What this means to the believer today is that God is not surprised by our weaknesses, questions and struggles. *Yada'* also means to discern or be aware of circumstances that affect a subject. This means that God has already discerned how the events of our lives will affect us.

The Father was quite aware of Jeremiah's age and experience; the Father was aware of the spiritual state of Israel; the Father was aware of the political climate; and the Father was aware of Jeremiah's temperament, zeal and flaws. The Father's discernment is so keen that he was able to weave all of those threads together for his glory.

The Father has discerned *our* situation too—he will weave together our flaws, our gifts, our opportunities, our environment and our calling so as to prepare and present us for his cause. So the big question is not whether or not God still loves us, but rather, whether we will love him enough to believe these truths and give our sins and struggles over to him.

LIKE A NURSING MOTHER

The nature of God is to be like a nursing mother to us: tender, focused, protective, adoring, nurturing.

This means that the Father will never ever leave or forsake us. Ever! Isaiah 49:15 reads: "Can a mother forget the baby at her breast / and have no compassion on the child she has borne? Though she may forget, / I will not forget you!"

When a mother nurses, as she focuses on her child, she may have a temporary memory loss. A hormone is released in moms when they are breastfeeding (or pumping their milk) that aids them in avoiding being overwhelmed by motherhood. When released, this hormone causes the mother to shut out the world around her and to shut down mentally—hence the temporary memory loss—so as to focus only on the little one who is in need of her undivided attention.

When a mother has difficulty with her milk supply while pumping, she is encouraged to focus on a photo of her baby. The photo will stimulate the brain and increase her milk supply almost instantly.

God is awesome! Notice, in the Isaiah passage, God does not compare himself to a proud father but rather to a nursing mother. Something very physiological occurs when a mother holds her child at her breast. It would be hard to imagine a mother holding her baby, hearing her child cry, having her milk supply stimulated, and still ignoring, denying and neglecting the child's needs. Yet even though this might happen, the Father goes on to say that he will never forget his children or their needs.

Our praise, our presence, our lives are all snapshots that stimulate the Father's supply of "milk" or daily bread for our life. We can't continue to run from the Father when we stumble. We must run to the Father when we're weak. Our sincere prayer and adoration allow his memory of our sin to be erased, and we have his undivided attention.

OUR NURTURING FATHER IS WAITING

> I praise you because I am fearfully and wonderfully made;
>   your works are wonderful. . . .
> My frame was not hidden from you
>   when I was made in the secret place.
> When I was woven together in the depths of the earth,
>   your eyes saw my unformed body. . . .
> How precious to me are your thoughts, O God!
>   How vast is the sum of them! (Psalm 139:14-17)

In this psalm, the writer is worshiping God for the wonderful thoughts and energy that went into creating humans. The Hebrew word for "fearfully" in this passage is *yare'*, which means a feeling of awe, reverence or holy respect, evoking a response that is usually worshipful. This is not to say that God "worships" his people. Yet God's love for and knowledge of us, even before we were formed in our mother's womb, was so exhilarating that it resulted in creation! Our existence is the result of the Father's wonderfully awesome brainstorming session. The thoughts of God concerning us are bountiful and beautiful, countless and endless, powerful and purposeful, euphoric and unique.

Psalm 139:14-17 is very similar to Jeremiah 1:5 in that the writer talks about the Father's knowledge of us prior to our being formed in our mother's womb. The Father has been patiently awaiting our arrival, our life and ministry. If the Father gets this much joy out of merely thinking about us, can you imagine his ecstasy the day we were born? I would even venture to say that the Father rejoices over us each morning when we awake (Zephaniah 3:17).

As we consider the truth of these passages and allow them to speak to our heart, we become better witnesses when we have the opportunity to invite people into a relationship with a living and loving Father who loves and forgives the lost and the found. Let nothing separate you from this kind of love; let nothing separate you from this kind of Father.

It is not possible for the Father to abandon us. His love is too great to allow him to forget those who mean the world to him.

Even when our heart is broken, even when our soul is wounded, and even when our world is turned upside down, it does not mean that God has forgotten about us. He can't. The Father loves us too much to forget us.

So although bad things happen to good people, it doesn't mean that God has abandoned me. It must simply mean that God sees things that I cannot see. He understands things that I cannot understand. It means that Father knows best.

It is very easy for me to feel abandoned by God when things do not go according to "the plan." I live so fully in the moment that it is almost impossible to believe that today's pain can bring tomorrow's victory. This is why trusting God is so important. I am learning to trust that the Father's nature will not allow him to turn away from me. His nature is not vengeful, harsh, mean-spirited or dreadful. Therefore I shouldn't expect these attributes from the Father.

"We are . . . persecuted, but not abandoned" (2 Corinthians 4:8-9). Being down doesn't mean that we're out.

Having experienced abandonment in my early life doesn't give me the right to expect the same treatment from my heavenly Father. He wants me to see something different when I look to him.

And he knew what that would cost me.

A sister in Christ comforted me after our second loss. She and her husband had just lost twins and could empathize with us. I'll never forget her words to me as she sensed my feeling of abandonment: "Your daughters are in heaven beholding the face of Jesus. How can God forget you with such beautiful reminders in his presence?"

Amen!

8

MYTHS WE CHOOSE TO BELIEVE ABOUT GOD

Who is God?

In the movie *Inherit the Wind*, the lawyer who defends the accused evolution teacher, Bert Cates, states, "God created humanity, and in all fairness humanity then returned the favor." Henry Drummond was saying that God is a figment of the human imagination. The story of creation, he'd say, was really the other way around. People, out of their inability to accept their own sovereignty, created a god to whom they could ascribe sovereignty and divinity.

I am often tempted to play God with God. God is sovereign and has created us for his pleasure. However, I work very subtly to form an image of God that suits me and my selfish pleasures. I make deals with God that he never agrees to.

It's sad to realize how I have assumed that God would grant me certain things in return for spiritual acts I would perform for him. How could I have based my actions on such one-sided conversations? I was diligently striving to keep a covenant with God, who hadn't so much as "pinky-sworn" or crossed his heart to such an arrangement. Yet I lived each day as though he had. When and how did the Almighty Creator become reduced to being my genie?

ENCOUNTER ON THE EMMAUS ROAD

The disciples' meeting with Jesus on the Emmaus Road can help us understand our false conceptions of God and his agenda. Much of the anguish and despair that are evident in Cleopas and the other disciple arose from a misconception of who Jesus was and what he actually came to do.

"Now that same day two of them were going to a village called Emmaus, about seven miles from Jerusalem" (Luke 24:13). Jesus had clearly instructed the disciples to meet him in Galilee, but the road to Emmaus was taking them in a different direction. It looks as though these two (we don't know if the other disciple is a woman or a man; some scholars believe it is Cleopas's wife) are returning home or going to some other safe place of retreat. Maybe they are going to see family, friends and familiar faces. Or perhaps like Peter and some of the other disciples who decided to return to their careers as fishermen, Cleopas is returning to a surer way of life—something more familiar to him. They certainly are not headed to Galilee. They are getting away from the pain and disappointment of life and ministry. They had offered Jesus so much time, energy and wisdom, and this is the thanks they've gotten: being left high and dry.

> As they talked and discussed these things with each other, Jesus himself came up and walked along with them; but they were kept from recognizing him.
>
> He asked them, "What are you discussing together as you walk along?"

They stood still, their faces downcast. (Luke 24:15-17)

Instead of meeting Jesus and the other disciples, these two are walking and stewing. Maybe they are heading to Emmaus because they were fearful for their lives in Jerusalem. Perhaps they don't want to be reminded of Jesus' sad death. Or of their own sad lives now that Jesus has died.

Jesus, knowing full well what has saddened them, asks, "What's up?"

They vent with this "stranger" and tell him everything:

We had hoped that he was the one who was going to redeem Israel. And what is more, it is the third day since all this took place. In addition, some of our women amazed us. They went to the tomb early this morning but didn't find his body. (Luke 24:21-23)

They tell everything they feel. Everything they think. Everything they've dreamed. Their whole story. They tell him everything except for how they arrived at that destination.

How did they arrive there?

WHAT LED THEM TO EMMAUS

The past week and a half had been very eventful. Just a week ago Jesus finally "came out of the closet" and admitted to the world who he really is. Jesus did several things that were firsts even for him.

He raised Lazarus from the dead, after four days, out in the open in front of everyone. The city was shaken. A lot of people put their trust in Jesus because of what he did for Lazarus. In fact, the officials now began plotting to kill Lazarus *and* Jesus: Jesus because he had the audacity to raise a man from the dead, Lazarus because he wouldn't shut his trap about the miracle.

Knowing all this, Jesus had his disciples borrow a donkey, and he rode it into Jerusalem during a huge feast. Out in the open, in front of everyone.

The people poured out of their houses and left their water jugs, gardening tools and livestock to see what all the commotion was about. The community was curious to see why the roads were lined with women waving palm branches and why dads had young cheerleaders on their shoulders. What was going on?

Jesus had arrived.

There is some debate over what Jesus was trying to communicate by riding into town on a donkey. Some say that he was demonstrating his humility by riding a beast of burden. Others have said that it was customary for sons of kings to ride on donkeys. Regardless, he knew that he was drawing a lot of attention by doing it. And as he went along, people began to throw their clothes on the road before him and cry out their hosannas in very loud voices. In fact, some of the religious leaders asked him to silence his fans. And the same Jesus who had previously shunned public praise stated that worshiping him was inevitable at this point.

"I tell you," he replied, "if they keep quiet, the stones will cry out." (Luke 19:40)

His procession welcomed the fanfare he'd previously shunned. These folks had seen him before. He was no stranger to their community. He must've had a different air about him this time: a boldness, a savvy, a confidence that the crowds had never seen before. In the past he had performed medical miracles but asked his patients to keep it all a secret. One time he even hid in the crowd from religious officials who threatened to kill him for performing a miracle on the

Lord's Day. And once he escaped when a crowd tried to crown him as their king after witnessing a tremendous and miraculous act.

Crown him—crown him. . . . Hmmm. . . . That's what they wanted to do to him: crown him.

They wanted a man they could crown. They had waited so long and so patiently for a benevolent king. So they cheered him and lauded him and encouraged him. "Hosanna!" they screamed. "Blessed is he who comes in the name of the Lord!" was their chant.

Apparently, they didn't know Jesus or his heavenly plans. So they cheered him as he rode into the Holy City. Finally their hope had arrived—or had it?

Ironically, the man they wanted to crown today was the same man they'd crucify tomorrow.

Why?

Because like Cleopas—and like me when I created God in my own image, for my own selfish purposes—they hoped he would be their answer to life. Instead, he was God's answer to spiritual death.

They hoped he would restore the sovereign state of Israel. Instead, he was restoring them and us to God.

They hoped he would end the Roman occupation. Instead, he ended Satan's occupation of our souls.

They hoped he would end the awful taxation and discrimination. They hoped he would bring all of his miracles into the royal palace. They hoped he would make life good. Real good.

Now here I have to come clean. I used to read this passage with smugness and arrogance. I'd ask myself, *How could people use Jesus like that?* With righteous disgust I would affirm my great faith and pat myself on the back for loving Jesus and serving Jesus so faithfully. I did this until *my* personal parade came to a grinding halt.

I often struggled to understand why the losses of Victoria and

Alexis were so traumatic for me. Of course there were the obvious reasons. We lost a child—twice. We were denied something that we thought was our inalienable right. Yet I knew that something else was gnawing deep at my soul, my faith and my sanity. My trauma affected my life on three fronts: faith, faithfulness and fatherhood.

Faith

Because I was raised in a Pentecostal tradition, I had a high regard for and sensitivity to the movement of the Holy Spirit. I learned that the unseen is much more powerful and meaningful than the seen. I also had an inquisitive mind that appreciated scholarship. My heart was trained to follow my intuitions and discernment in order to know and obey God. My mind challenged me to understand Scripture and theology. Further, I had an affinity for high church liturgy because of its symbolism, and its reverential approach to worship appealed to my imagination and creativity. This is why I enjoyed worshiping with Presbyterian and Episcopalian friends.

I often asked myself if I was a Pentecostal trapped inside an evangelical mind. Or was I an evangelical who had been set free by the Spirit? Pentecostalism appealed to my soul. Evangelicalism appealed to my intellect. Liturgical worship appealed to my imagination. I often felt like a "Pentegelical" or "Presbycostal."

My understanding of Pentecostals was that we have a very high regard for the movement of the Spirit. We believe in the gifts of the Spirit, exuberant worship and miraculous spiritual encounters. The Spirit is the presence of God on the Earth today. My understanding of evangelicals was that they have a very high view of Scripture and see it as infallible, which means it is much more reliable than "sensing" an unction or nudge from the Spirit.

Never feeling quite at home in either tradition, in college I ventured out and participated in the Word of Faith movement. Some have described this sect of Christianity as "name-it-claim-it theology" or "health-and-wealth" ministries. (I don't wish to be negative or pejorative by using such terms.) The Word of Faith movement appealed to me because it had a high regard for both the Word of God and the power of God. Its doctrine certainly highlighted the miraculous work of the Spirit—and I like that. And there was definitely a reverence for God's holiness and splendor—and I like that too. Word of Faith theology engaged my heart, intellect and imagination—and I really liked that.

The Word of Faith movement taught me that if I could find God's promise to me in Scripture, regardless of the context, I could believe in that promise. In fact, I could receive all of God's best blessings if I would just believe with my heart and confess scriptural truths with my mouth.

Now, I believe that there is some real truth in this teaching. However, my new theology didn't make room for the sovereignty of God. There were certain things that God just wouldn't do—*and it was not due to a lack of faith*. He merely has a different plan.

Unfortunately, my new faith journey led me down some dangerous roads. I thought that "faith" was my answer to everything. If I merely had enough faith, I'd move the heart of God. If I had enough faith, I'd move mountains and witness (and perform) miracles.

As a young man, I found that life was pretty good to me. I had been called into ministry at the very early age of fifteen. I had a degree from a prestigious university. I fell in love with and married a beautiful woman whom I met in college. I assumed that all these blessings were merely the result of confessing all the right Scriptures for many years.

The true Jesus who died for me and who has a plan for my life was much different, though, from the imaginary "Jesus" whom I'd created for my own plans. I think this was true for Cleopas too. Perhaps that is why he didn't recognize the true Jesus. I didn't recognize him either on my sad road.

FAITHFULNESS

I had become a Christian as an eleven-year-old. I have always believed in God. Always. Many adult leaders and mentors assured me that they sensed God's hand and call on my life. In the African American church tradition, that usually means you are going to preach. Since all this was determined, I was admonished to commit myself totally to the things of God. My mentors taught me to abstain from sex, and I did. They taught me not to partake of alcohol and tobacco, and I didn't. I was instructed to avoid worldly activities like attending movies and high school mixers, and I avoided them even though I was on homecoming court and I was captain of the track team in high school.

I had a good track record, and I obeyed God. I assumed I was scoring heavenly brownie points by being so good.

Losing our daughters made me feel that everything that I had done for Christ was for nothing. I felt duped. Stupid. Used. I understood how bad things happen to bad people. However, I didn't understand how and why bad things happen to good people. I asked myself, *Why have I served God so faithfully if this is my reward?* Had my faithfulness itself been a secret negotiation with God, an attempt to bribe him? I gave God the best years of my life—years that people would kill to have again. My youth! And it would appear that his response was "So what!"

It was enough to put me on my personal road to Emmaus.

FATHERLESSNESS

Although I saw my father from time to time, his absence left a very major wound in my heart and soul. My mother eventually remarried; my stepfather was a hard worker, but he remained very distant emotionally. To make matters worse, he had very low self-esteem because, while growing up in Mississippi, he had had to drop out of elementary school to work as a sharecropper with his family. This contributed to his emotional distance from me—he felt that he had nothing to offer a bright, inquisitive stepson. So I had two fathers, neither of whom ever paid me much attention, and I concluded that something was wrong with me.

As a result of all of this, I developed very low self-esteem and felt that I was never manly enough or smart enough or athletic enough to fit in with my peers. There was no man in my life to tell me anything to the contrary. In many ways I felt invisible. In my adolescence, the only way I could make sense of my pain and insecurity was to believe that if I only had a father who invested in me, I could have been smarter, more popular, more confident, more athletic and tougher. To some extent this is probably true.

As a married man, I told myself that I could compensate for not having a father by becoming one. I figured since all of my greatest wounds seemed to have come from the lack of guidance and protection of a father or father-figure, I could reverse all of my hurts by becoming the world's best dad.

I was convinced that fatherhood was going to surgically remove every bad thing that had ever happened to me. But the surgery was called off. At the same time I was trying to comfort my wife who felt as though she had failed me.

I had a huge theological crisis on my hands. No one understood my pain, because I couldn't explain it. All I knew was that

• the pain of fatherlessness that I'd hidden for years had sprung up like a released beach ball that had been held underwater.

- I felt used by God. He didn't hold up his end of the bargain and therefore could not be trusted any longer.

- maybe he could be trusted, but I was deemed so vile that he too, my heavenly Father, had turned on me. I was no longer special to him.

All my life, God was the One I ran to when my heart was torn in pieces. Who do you run to when it's God who mistreats you?

THE LONELY ROAD

I understand Cleopas and the other disciple completely! What a lonely and misunderstood road they traveled. And what makes the road so lonely is that it is a road *they* chose to travel—not God. Jesus never promised that he would not die. He never promised me that by having the right faith or being faithful I'd get everything I prayed for or that I would be a dad. Cleopas and I got our wires crossed somehow. We both assumed too much, and we both wound up devastated.

> The next day the great crowd that had come for the Feast heard that Jesus was on his way to Jerusalem. They took palm branches and went out to meet him, shouting,
>   "Hosanna!"
>   "Blessed is he who comes in the name of the Lord!"
>   "Blessed is the King of Israel!" (John 12:12-13)

Boy, were they in for a rude awakening—*a big one!* Jesus was about to take a detour—*a big one!*

The parade was about to end. Why? Because everyone (including the disciples) thought that Jesus was going to overthrow Rome. However, when he should have turned right and headed toward Rome, he turned left—toward Calvary.

Golgotha. It means the place of the skull.

Death. A death to which Jesus would surrender.

Ugh!

Why would he turn in that direction? He wouldn't be so careless, thoughtless and cruel to have recruited all those followers just to desert them, would he? Maybe he couldn't handle the pressure. Maybe he was afraid of success.

Or maybe he had to be about his Father's business!

And what a peculiar business it was: loving prostitutes, touching lepers, befriending Samaritans, hugging children, respecting women, training fishermen to preach and heal, and breaking the heart of everyone he loves just to save them.

He was very faithful to his Father's business, even when his friends and fans didn't like it. And soon the noisy cheerleaders would appease the Pharisees by silencing their own praise.

He was merely a means to their long-awaited end. The crowds had no idea of what Jesus was really about or who he really was. The crowds thought that Jesus was their long-awaited king who would finally free Israel from the oppressive powers of Rome. They saw Jesus exclusively through their own selfish lenses.

How many times did he say he would die? How many times did he dodge their praise? How many times did he say that he was not of this world? Why did they still insist on making him their king? And why didn't the crowd want to be part of his kingdom?

Stop!

All of a sudden the parade comes to a screeching halt. Folks are bumping into the people in front of them. What is going on? Where is Jesus going?

"Hey, that's not the way to Rome, Jesus!"

"Hey, Jesus, we don't want you to go that way!"

"Hey, that's not what we signed up for, Jesus!"

"Hey, Jesus, that's the way to Golgotha!"

"Can't he do anything right?"

The people gasped. And the crowds thinned. Jesus had only teased them. He wasn't going to be their king after all—mainly because they refused to be part of his kingdom.

When we recognize the King, we recognize his kingdom. When we ignore the King, we forfeit the kingdom. We cannot have it both ways in Christ. The crowds didn't really want his kingdom because they didn't respect him as king. They only followed him when they thought they liked where he was going.

We are no different. We are not better.

We have confused our personal greed with our spiritual need. Some of us believe that Jesus lived and died just to endorse spiritualization of the American dream.

Following Jesus' parade is about laying down our inalienable rights, not demanding them.

It is not Christ who abandons us—we abandon him. And it isn't for good reasons either. He doesn't lie. He doesn't break covenants. He doesn't go back on his word. He is only guilty of doing what's best for his kingdom and his subjects. But we dislike his decisions and distrust his motives.

MEETING AT THE CROSS

The only way we can find Christ again is to meet him at the cross. We can only bear our cross when we understand that even Jesus was subject to suffering and the perfect will of our heavenly Creator. So if Jesus went to the cross ever so willingly, what makes us think that we have the right to avoid it?

Golgotha.

Death.

A death to which our desires must surrender.

A death to which our dreams must surrender.

A death to which our self-proclaimed rights must surrender.

Ugh!

If he is our King, we must be his entourage *everywhere* he goes.

Why do we follow Jesus? What did we sign up for? What do we expect from God? Time will tell.

Jesus, our King, refused to let the praises of his subjects keep him from subjecting himself to humiliation, rejection and execution. Jesus refused to play a role in the fantasies of his very fickle public. He was not marching to the beat of their praise. He was marching obediently to the beat of the Father's plan.

Jesus broke all the rules by refusing to play their games. He was not responsible for their self-centered, one-sided contracts. By his refusal, he shattered their myths about who he was and what he'd do. And he continues to shatter these myths today.

Jesus' commitment is to the big picture of the kingdom. He is not interested in a starring role in our mythological dramas.

9

WHAT'S ALL THE HYPE ABOUT GRACE IF I STILL HAVE TO SUFFER?

My poem called "Grace":

I *know* grace, but I don't understand it.
Grace eludes me and embraces me, all at the same time.
When I try to justify my sins of arrogance, fear, disobedience,
    sinfulness, pride and idolatry, grace eludes me . . .
And when I admit my arrogance, fear, disobedience, sinfulness,
    pride and idolatry, grace embraces me.

I *have received* grace, but I don't understand it.
It ignores me and acknowledges me, all at the same time.
When I try to do good on my own, grace seems to cover her
    yawning mouth in a *not-so-impressed* manner.
However, the more I fall, the more grace seems to run to my aid,
    lifting me out of my own mire, asking if I am all right.

I *experience* grace, but I don't understand it.
It defeats me and sustains me, all at the same time.

When I try to convince God that he should go easy on me, grace reminds me that he already has—at Calvary.

But when I try to beat myself up and prove to God my guilt and unworthiness and that I should be punished, grace reminds me that I *was* gruesomely and vicariously punished at Calvary—via Jesus' substitutionary death.

I *feel* grace, but I don't understand it.

It disqualifies me and qualifies me, all at the same time.

When I feel that I should be recognized for a great sermon, idea or prayer, I am reminded that God is my source.

And when I am accused of my countless failures, I am reminded that God alone is my judge—not me, not Satan, not anyone else.

I receive grace, but I don't get it.

I experience grace, but I can't fathom it.

I feel grace, but I don't comprehend it.

I know grace, but I still don't understand it.

Lord,

Though I don't get it

Though I can't fathom it

Though I don't comprehend it

And though I don't understand it . . .

Thank you, Lord, for your amazing grace that allows you to fully love and forgive your children even when we can't fully love or forgive ourselves.

Amen.

What Grace Isn't

Due to my own bad theology and some goods I was sold by our quick-fix culture, I was suffering from a gross misunderstanding of the concept of grace. What I learned on the Emmaus Road is what grace *is not.*

Grace is not God's willingness to wink at our sinfulness with a nonchalant type of boys-will-be-boys attitude.

Grace is not a spiritual crutch that allows us to break God's heart and destroy our lives just because we say, "Sorry, God," afterward.

Grace is not a spiritual prophylactic that protects us from the repercussions of our disobedient actions.

Grace is not a lovesick God who can't help but ignore our sinfulness.

Grace is not blind.

Grace is not cheap.

Grace does not debilitate; rather it empowers.

On the other hand, grace is like

- the cotton swab on the end of the Q-Tip that protects my ear from the hard Q-Tip stick

- a spare tire that helps me to drive to the nearest auto mechanic shop where I can find help

- a safety net that helps to catch me when I lose my footing

- a sling, or cast, or brace that comforts, stabilizes and secures until my renewed strength kicks in

Grace empowers rather than debilitates.

God Is with Us

Jesus was called Immanuel, which means "God is with us." And Immanuel came to bring salvation to the world. Salvation means wholeness, health, hope and strength.

Immanuel came to do something more beautiful than merely taking away all our worries and heartaches. Immanuel came to embrace us in the midst of our life's storms and turmoil, because Immanuel couldn't stand to see us endure such hardship all alone.

Therefore, God's gift of grace is not an escape from pain but rather his ability to embrace us in the midst of our pain. Salvation is not an escape from life and its pains but rather an engagement with the hurting world. God became flesh in order to engage himself with the hurts and hurting of this life.

This is grace—God's unmerited favor. And what is more favorable than to have God's presence no matter where we go or what we go through?

Grace is God's unearned favor and constant abiding presence during the roughest spots of life.

We need his grace. I certainly do!

When we mistake God's grace for something that it is not, we set ourselves up for great disappointment and frustration. Grace is the space that God gives us to back up, ask for strength and reapproach our situation differently. Grace was not designed for those who want to continue making the same mistakes. It was designed for frail but relentless humans who need the space to try and try again until they are able to appropriately apply God's strength to their struggle-filled life.

If God is offering grace, we will surely need it.

Jesus gave Peter a powerful message right after he was restored: "I have prayed for you, Simon, that your faith may not fail" (Luke 22:32). On one hand, Jesus was encouraging Peter. On the other hand, he was informing Peter of how he would die. He offered Peter soothing words of grace because he would need them one day.

So when the Lord tells us that he will never leave us or forsake us, he isn't promising us the absence of hardship. In fact, hardship is a given: "Everyone who wants to live a godly life in Christ Jesus will be persecuted" (2 Timothy 3:12). The comfort that the Lord offers is his promises to grant us his presence in the midst of our hardships.

Grace is almost a promise that struggle is near. Grace is also a promise that the love and comfort and strength of God are even nearer.

Remember, the absence of hardship doesn't build character. The absence of trouble doesn't build faith. The absence of heartache doesn't make us empathic.

I am who I am because of grace. Were it not for grace, I would have crumbled miserably during the rocky times of life. Grace has not only purchased salvation for me; it weaves the very character and attributes of our holy God into the fibers of my soul so that I inch toward becoming and acting more and more like him. Character and identity are shaped by grace.

Because of grace, I can do more than look at Jesus' cross. I can bear my own cross and become numb to the siren song of this world.

Because of amazing grace, I can do more than merely sing of it. I become a song and psalm to the Lord as grace teaches me to pray, "Not my will, but yours be done."

Were it not for God's grace, I might've given up on faith, turned away from God or walked away from the only authentic power I know. Grace wouldn't let me stray too far.

TAKING A SWING AT GOD

My mother says that as a toddler I had a temper. If I fell, I'd hit her on the leg or arm. If another child hit me, I'd run to her and hit her. Mom said that although I didn't have the verbal language to articulate my feelings, she knew full well what I was trying to say. "Why won't you help me? Didn't you see me fall? Why didn't you pick me up?

You're supposed to protect me from falls like that!"

To my embarrassment, I must admit that when life hits me hard or I stumble and fall, I swing at God. Whether it's with prayerlessness or emotional distance, I try my best to let God know that he missed an opportunity to help me. After our loss of Victoria and Alexis, I tried to push God away. I went beyond accusing him of not helping me; I started to accuse God of being the one who was attacking me.

I tried to walk away, but grace wouldn't allow it. I tried to upset God with angry prayers and mean journal entries, but grace ignored them. It was as if Jesus understood and prayed, "Father, forgive them, for they do not know what they are doing . . ." (Luke 23:34).

Grace made me as helpless and dumbfounded as the high priest's servant who thought he could overpower and arrest Jesus in the Garden of Gethsemane. Trying to defend his Master, Peter sliced off the man's ear. But Jesus was still willing to show grace to his enemies—he healed his assailant's severed ear. Then Jesus surrendered his wrists to the man so that he could continue his arrest.

Grace makes me love that snapshot of Jesus! This story tells me that Jesus would never, under *any* circumstances, choose to become my enemy.

And since he isn't my enemy, he must be on my side. So when I wanted him to leave, his grace caused him to stay. The only reason I can stand for him and cling to him is that he refuses to let go of me. It is his grip, not mine, that keeps us connected.

When I was a small child, my world revolved around my mother. I wouldn't have hurt her for anything in the world. She understood that. She knew that for me to lash out at her meant that I was in pain or was afraid, and I couldn't articulate it.

Grace told Jesus how much I love him. He knew that I didn't have the ability to articulate the incredible pain in my soul. Grace allowed me to eventually stop fighting against Jesus and to begin fighting *with* him. I realized that I would rather go to hell and back with Jesus than to experience great prosperity without him.

So I stood when evil and torment were all around me and inside of me. And it was not because my legs were strong. I stood because God's grace was amazing to me.

If grace shielded us from life's tears, heartache and disappointment, we would have no occasion for faith, perseverance and prayer.

Grace not only allows us to see who we are under pressure; it allows us to see who we are when God stands beside us during the dark night of our souls. Grace helps us to appreciate the work of the Father within us.

Grace looks beyond what we want and prepares us for what we need in order to become who we were created to be.

The miracle of grace is not that God stops the storms of life. The miracle of grace is that he's willing to stay in the boat with us during the storms of life.

God is charting my course, even when I am too stubborn to acknowledge my need for him to be my captain.

This is what makes grace so amazing.

PRAYER OF TRANSFORMATION

"What can I offer the LORD
  for all he has done for me?"
    (Psalm 116:12 NLT)

Father,
Please forgive my sins of presumed entitlement: the sins of pride, arrogance, disobedience, insincerity, selfishness and lust that I commit in light of my own presumed goodness. These are the sins I commit when I think that you owe me something in return for my "wonderfully faithful" service

to you. You owe me nothing! I owe you everything because you have offered me everything, including your dear Son and heaven.

Please honor my prayer, Lord, by changing my heart, my will and my response to you. Give me a praying spirit. Give me a loving spirit. Give me a faithful spirit. Please empower me by giving me your Holy Spirit without measure.

I will arise to meet you with a humbled heart. You still resist the proud and you still give grace to the humble. Have mercy, Lord, on your child and help me to trust and obey you. Amen.

SECTION THREE

A METHOD

TO GOD'S

MADNESS

10

WHAT GOD DOES
WITH THE BAD STUFF

I hate Christianese! That is, the archaic jargon and religious words used by Christians. It is so easy to quote Scriptures and clichés without understanding them—or believing them. We toss these words around a lot in Christendom, and most people don't have a clue as to what they really mean.

Redemption is one of those words. I've sung about it. I've even preached about it. I was aware of the Scriptures that talk about it. But I had no clue about what it meant to live it.

Here's how I learned to understand and appreciate this mystical concept.

THE MEANING OF REDEMPTION

One day I watched a television commercial in which a six- or seven-year-old girl was standing next to a garbage can. I can still hear her little voice thanking everyone for helping to save the life of her dad, a police officer. At first I thought it was a 911 commercial or a call for a neighborhood watch program. Instead it was a commercial about trash.

The little girl went on to say that because the people of her community had been willing to recycle, her dad was alive and well. She explained that milk containers and other forms of plastic are sometimes recycled and used to make bulletproof vests for police officers. Her dad was wearing one of the milk-containers-turned-bulletproof-vests, and it saved his life.

One person's recyclable trash is another person's bulletproof vest!

Environmentally minded individuals performed their civic duty of recycling their bottles, tins, aluminum, paper and plastic, never giving a thought to what these things would become in their next life. Someone melted this junk and reshaped it into something worthwhile—a bulletproof vest.

Redemption means nothing more than to reuse or recycle something for a different purpose, the higher purpose of God.

Now, this concept of redemption was foreign to me. I mainly came to Christ in order to avoid "junk" in my life. I wanted to circumvent pain, conflict, heartache, disappointment and loss. Not having to deal with all that crap would've been true redemption for me. (What Bible was I reading?)

In a million years, I would never have thought that God would "endorse" pain by using it for his desired outcome in my life. I didn't have the patience or theology for such nonsense. So I honestly don't know what I was thinking as I sang to and taught about our great Redeemer. I supposed that redemption just meant that Jesus was my kinsman and had purchased the rights to my life with his precious blood. I didn't understand that Jesus purchased my life, my pain, my history, my scars and my brokenness—and he is yet redeeming all of it.

It's amazing. I have been redeemed and I am still being redeemed. I have been saved and I am still being saved.

For over twenty-five years I have studied the historical meaning of Christ's cross. It is only recently that I have come to understand the full benefit of redemption that was purchased on the cross.

Redemption is proof of our Father's sovereignty. Only someone who is sovereign could observe our pain at any given moment, fully sympathize with us, and at the same time fully understand when and where that painful experience would greatly benefit us—and glorify him.

Suppose you and I have a coupon for free food or merchandise. The paper that the coupon is printed on is virtually worthless. In fact, if we were to take the coupon to a bank and ask for the equivalent value in cash, we'd be laughed at—or arrested. The coupon is valued or recognized only by the corporation that has offered to redeem it. Everywhere else, the piece of paper is just a piece of junk!

Likewise, our brokenness looks like junk to most people. Our scars and disappointments seem to be good for nothing until we place them in the hands of the One who offers to redeem them. Our Redeemer is sovereign. He can take anything that looks broken and fix it like new. He can bring good out of any situation that he is invited into.

BIBLICAL PICTURES OF REDEMPTION

The Bible is full of redemption stories.

Moses fled Egypt after it became public that he had murdered an Egyptian. He spent forty years on the backside of a mountain. Was this wasted time? Or did God use this time as preparation for the future? Did this experience help Moses to understand the terrain better so that he could lead hundreds of men, women and children out of Egypt and through the wilderness?

Joseph was a dreamer who recounted his dreams to family members. Jealousy burned in the hearts of Joseph's brothers, and they sold him into slavery. After seasons of abuse, abandonment, conspiracy, attempted seduction and incarceration, God raised Joseph to a place of political prominence. When the family was reunited, Joseph told his brothers that what they had intended for his harm, God used for his good.

Paul experienced great discomfort that he wanted the Father to address. After all, he had witnessed and experienced many miracles in his ministry; surely God would want to deliver Paul and give him a pain-free life. "To keep me from becoming conceited because of these surpassingly great revelations, there was given me a thorn in my flesh, a messenger of Satan, to torment me. Three times I pleaded with the Lord to take it away from me" (2 Corinthians 12:7-8). Paul wanted God to see things his way and heal him of this particular "thorn." The Father's response reflects the tone of a sovereign Redeemer: "But he said to me, 'My grace is sufficient for you, for my power is made perfect in weakness' " (2 Corinthians 12:9).

Strength in Weakness

I struggled beneath the weight of my hardships because of what I believed they represented. In my estimation, a hardship meant that God was getting even with me about something. I thought hardship meant that God had abandoned me—after many years of faithful service. But Paul's writings shed new light for me.

How could God forget me in my weakness, if that is when and where his strength is revealed?

Any strength I obtained that was not his strength would not last. His strength only shows up when our own strength fails us.

My greatest fear in life had been that God would abandon me.

That is why from early on I was determined to become a model Christian—I decided to win God over!

I hate to see my own weaknesses. In my world, weakness meant I would be disqualified from life's best blessings. Weakness meant I was unworthy of the blessings and benefits that only the "strong" receive. Therefore, I made a point of being strong and in control—even if that was the furthest thing from the truth. Perhaps I felt that my weaknesses would disappoint God and he would lose faith in me if he knew about them.

I do have many weaknesses, but God has never disowned me. His response to my weaknesses has been a tremendous outpouring of grace. Just think, I expected his worst and he offered me his best. In fact, I never saw God's best until he saw my worst. God saw my garbage, and he was willing to recycle it into something incredibly useful. Jesus not only saves, he recycles. And the redeemed of the Lord should say so (Psalm 107:2)!

11

FAITH, FRAGMENTS AND FIRE

Although it stills pains me to utter such words, God does bring good out of bad.

For years I was convinced that God was interested in Christian output. The more we did, the happier he was. As a result of this erroneous view, I always pushed like mad to get from point A to point B faster than anyone else. I believed that point B made God happy, and it made me look like a wonderful super-Christian. I ascribed absolutely no value to the journey between points A and B.

But Christian faith is not about arriving. It is about journeying with the Savior.

I wish someone had told me. Or I wish I had listened when someone did actually tell me.

PAUL'S VOYAGE

Acts 27 offers a prime example of how God can use broken fragments in order to save our lives. The apostle Paul was a prisoner on his way to trial so that he could stand before and appeal to Caesar. The ship that transported the prisoners encountered difficult weather. His captors transferred him to another ship headed to Ethiopia. A strong wind beat up the ship. In fact, Paul warned his captors not to try to find another port, but they didn't listen to him. They should have! The men who were in charge of the boat were so worried and fearful that they threw their tackle overboard to lighten their load. The sailors tried to get the ship close to land, but the angry waters were too shallow.

Paul spoke up and said that they should have listened to him! He went on to say that he'd had a vision of an angel of the Lord. The angel in his vision offered hope that every person onboard would be spared, although the boat would suffer ruin. This was hard for the men to grasp, because they hadn't seen the sun for days and were very seasick. It was hard to listen to some criminal fanatic describing a conversation with an angel of God who could foretell the future.

The angel was right.

The ship attempted to dock, but it was too big. The closer it got to the shore, the more destruction it suffered. But although the ship was on course for a huge disaster, God was still in control of the wind, the sea, the captain and the prisoners onboard.

The ship could not get all the way to the shore because of the really shallow waters. Having endured a good beating from the wind and rocks, the ship broke apart and was beginning to sink. This seemed to be a dreaded end for everyone on board.

At first, the loyal guards prepared to kill the prisoners so that they wouldn't get away. Not on their watch! But the commanding officer spared all of the prisoners because he wanted to save Paul. He ordered that the prisoners be allowed to jump overboard and swim to safety. The nonswimmers were allowed to grab a plank of debris from the wounded ship and try their best to make it to shore. And just as God had promised Paul, no one died. Everyone made it ashore safely.

It had been a rough several weeks on the sea, and I am sure that Paul wanted to kiss the ground when he swam ashore to the island of Malta. The islanders were kind and built a fire to welcome the castaways. As Paul attempted to settle his heart and warm his soul, a poisonous snake jumped out of the fire and fastened itself on his hand.

Talk about a bad day! Can you imagine swimming for your life after a white-knuckle voyage on the high seas, just to have a snake jump out of the fire and bite you?

Everyone thought Paul must have been a very wicked man to deserve such a series of disasters in a single day. Paul, however, shook the snake into the fire with the ease you'd show in shaking a ladybug off your wrist.

Boy, did that capture the attention of the Maltans! Doors were immediately opened for Paul to offer powerful ministry on that island.

The head official of the island was so impressed with the power displayed by Paul that he invited this prisoner to his estate to minister to his father-in-law, who was ill. And soon a full revival broke out across the entire island. It wasn't a run-of-the-mill crowd of frenzied religious groupies. All of the sick people on the island came to Jesus, and they were healed (Acts 28:7-10).

Paul stayed there for three months. Just long enough for the damaged ship to be repaired, or long enough to finish God's mission. Whichever came first.

This story amazes me because it reflects God's tremendous ability to be our sovereign Redeemer. God can take something that purely looks like a fluke, a deviation from the desired path, a turn for the worse, and change it into something beautiful.

THE SHIP OF MY LIFE

The ship in the Acts account reflects parts of my life so well. The captain wanted to get his ship to the shore but couldn't due to shallow rocky waters. Although the ship couldn't get to shore in one piece, the shipmates and passengers did. And although the ship was broken, it provided the means by which the timid swimmers could find safety—broken planks. And then a revival broke out, and the gospel was preached to the residents of Malta Island.

This looks like a rendezvous with destiny! Could God have allowed this so that Paul could preach on this island? Is God that strategic? That wise? That good?

God obviously wanted Paul on that island—but without the ship. God never promised Paul that the ship would be saved. He only promised that every passenger would be.

This is where following God gets tricky.

I want to be saved—not just from my sins and eternal damnation. I want to be saved from heartache, depression, fear, discomfort, hunger, racism, loneliness, miscarriage, fatherlessness, unemployment and disappointment.

This is not what God saved us from, or for.

God saves *us*. Our future. Our destiny. He never promises us that our ship will be saved. Rather, he promises that we won't taste death.

The loss of our ship is not the same as the loss of our soul, although I sometimes confuse the two.

In many instances, it is the loss of our "ship" that allows many of us to "float" on the broken pieces into a more intimate relationship with the Lord. Or, in some cases, the brokenness is what brings us closer to the Lord.

My pain in experiencing fatherlessness led me in several unhealthy directions, including perfectionism and habitually seeking everyone's approval. It also led me to search for my heavenly Father.

I had intimate life-altering encounters with Jesus before most of my friends had even heard of him. I was intrigued with the notion of a divine God since I was four or five. God was giving me biblical insights in scriptural interpretation when I was eleven years old. (I rarely told anyone, because I figured if he was revealing it to a kid, everyone else at church must already know it.) I was leading my friends to Christ when I was twelve (two of these friends grew up to become ministers). But it all started with my pursuit of a father figure.

God saved my life. However, my ship suffered loss. That ship was my dreams, my agenda, my needs. But in the midst of my brokenness, God gave me the strength to hold on to one of those broken fragments and to float toward a destination that God had in mind for my life.

This is why Jesus is our great Redeemer—because he can take broken planks and let you use them to float to safety.

REINTERPRETING MY SUFFERING

I grew up praying that God would deliver me out of all my troubles. I figured that trials and tribulations were of the devil, so I asked Jesus to protect me from all of them. I saw nothing redemptive in sicknesses or hardships, so I rebuked anything that looked like it might cause me the least bit of discomfort.

When difficulty came, I was sure that was God "letting me have it."

The problem with feeling judged during rough times is that it must mean that I was being rewarded in the good times. Neither is true—not necessarily.

Allowing God to redefine the way we interpret our suffering may spare us considerable mental and emotional anguish.

JOSEPH: SEEING GOD AT WORK

In Genesis 37, Joseph was considered the great dreamer. His future was bright until his bragging rights wore thin on his brothers' nerves.

Maybe he was too boastful. Maybe he should've kept his mouth shut. We don't know. What we do know is that he suffered greatly at the hands of loved ones and was sold to a group of Ishmaelites. The Ishmaelites sold Joseph to an Egyptian official named Potiphar. Potiphar's wife tried to seduce Joseph, and when he didn't cave in to her whims, she lied and accused him of sexual assault. Joseph went to prison.

In prison Joseph was shown tremendous favor because God was clearly with him. "So the warden put Joseph in charge of all those held in the prison, and he was made responsible for all that was done there" (Genesis 39:22). Joseph was still in jail, but God's favor still rested on him. His present condition was not an indicator of God's love or God's plan for him.

God's favor and Joseph's gifts of interpreting dreams sprung him from jail. Joseph interpreted a key dream for Pharaoh and was immediately promoted to the number-two man in all of Egypt, although he was a foreigner.

When famine drove foreigners to Egypt for relief, Joseph's brothers were among them. Imagine their surprise—and horror—when Joseph revealed his identity to them. A vengeful man would have had them beheaded.

Lucky for them that Joseph wasn't a vengeful man. He comforted his brothers by saying, "You intended to harm me, but God intended it for good" (Genesis 50:20).

Joseph's spiritual favor was exceeded only by his spiritual maturity. Only a mature person could see God's blessings in the midst of a personal hell. Joseph's faith in and experience with God were so keen that he knew God must have had a purpose for allowing such a painful ordeal.

A healthy and biblically accurate concept of the Father gives us a healthy and biblically accurate concept of ourselves, his children. Joseph knew that God is strategically purposeful and wastes nothing, including time. So if one of God's children is suffering a great ordeal, God is too good to waste that. It must be for some hidden-but-soon-to-be-revealed plan: "And we know that in all things God works for the good of those who love him, who have been called according to his purpose" (Romans 8:28).

The Three Hebrew Men: Walking Through Fire

An interesting thing often occurs during our time of hardship: we grow! A new liberty often opens up during the rough times of our life. When we suffer, our focus changes, our paradigm shifts, and we prioritize and concentrate on what is truly important. I don't fully understand this phenomenon, I just believe it.

The story of the three Hebrew boys (Daniel 3:19-25) and their heroic faith is one of the most popular plots of the Bible, especially with children. I believe there is much that adults can glean from this powerful story too.

These three men were tossed into the fire because they refused to trust in a false god. They refused to dance to the rhythm of popular religious and political culture. Nebuchadnezzar ordered the furnace to be heated seven times hotter because these men had returned his flippant question ("What god will be able to rescue you from my hand?") with an equally flippant response: "Even if he doesn't choose to, he is able to!" They were bound hand and foot and thrown into the flames.

The furnace was so hot that the heat killed the guards who threw the three men into it. Yet as Nebuchadnezzar sat and waited to hear the moans and screams of the three men, he heard none. Then he became so sure that his eyes were deceiving him that he called trusted advisers to verify the number of men who had been banished to this fiery hell.

"Three, sir."

"Then why do I see four men walking around? The forth one looks angelic!" King Nebuchadnezzar ordered the men to come out so that he could question them.

No one untied them. They walked out on their own.

But they hadn't walked *in* on their own. They had been bound with ropes. Now the ropes were nowhere to be found.

Their hair didn't smell like smoke. Their clothes weren't charred. Their skin wasn't darkened with soot from the flames. Their lungs weren't full of deadly smoke and fumes. And the ropes that bound them had somehow dissipated in the fire.

Most people remember the miraculous rescue of the three men. This is the part that I always loved as a young Sunday school student. But as an adult I read Scripture for comfort and direction rather than intrigue and suspense. Two notable things occur to me in regard to this passage.

First, God's presence is with the men! They take a very bold and mature stance. They admit that they'd rather die than to bow to some false god. What conviction and integrity! They never equate service to God with a life that is free from suffering.

As much as I hate the thought that serving God means that I must suffer hardship, I hate the thought of suffering alone even more. This story helps me to shift a very major life paradigm by posing an important question: Do I live to avoid pain or to give God glory? Have I spiritualized comfort and prosperity? Do I rebuke trouble and call it evil? Or do I view hardship as something that comes to purge my soul of selfishness and its need for comfort?

The three men chose to suffer, and God chose to keep them company. I suppose that suffering can't be so awful if that is where God chooses to show up.

Second, the men come out the same way they went in, except for the ropes that bound their hands and feet. Perhaps the only things that experienced damage in the flames were the ropes that bound the men. This is just as amazing to me as the miraculous rescue.

ESCAPING OUR FURNACE

Maybe that is what happens to us—we make a choice to follow God. We ignore the invitations of false and temporal gods. We refuse to dance to the rhythm of popular opinion. And we don't care what price we pay for following our truest conviction: God loves us and is counting on us to requite his love.

And suddenly, seemingly out of nowhere, life happens to us: Sickness. Loss. Unemployment. Divorce. Death. Bankruptcy. Doubt.

Yet we survive. Somehow God's grace upholds us in the darkest nights, and we escape unscathed, practically.

You don't smell fire in our hair. You don't see charred clothing. You don't see singed hair. The only evidence that we've been in a "furnace" is the fact that old "ropes" of self-sufficiency, idolatry and pride no longer bind our hands and feet.

We don't care as much about what others think about us. We don't care as much about popularity. We don't care as much about making money. We are less judgmental and more compassionate. The darkness of the furnace has focused our eyes. The heat of the furnace has melted our pretension. And the flames of the furnace have burned up our ropes, so we experience a newfound liberty in Christ.

We rarely understand why God allows us to take the hits that we do. As Christians, we usually operate from the assumption that we are pure and innately righteous. On the contrary, we are very broken people who struggle with sin, arrogance and self-preoccupation. This is often demonstrated by the futile prayers we offer up to the Father: "Lord, please change my wife," "Lord, please change my employer," "Lord, please fix my pastor and help him/her to see things our way." You get my point.

We naturally assume that if there is a problem, it is the other person who needs to see the light. It is never our fault. In fact, we believe life would be much simpler if people would just get with our program! What if the fiery furnaces that we face are permitted so that the ropes that bind us can be burned off and utterly destroyed?

We often struggle because we feel that we don't deserve our fiery furnaces. Perhaps the fiery furnace is a means of God's providing us what we truly want: liberty from whatever binds us. Liberty is costly, but so is bondage.

Since we have to experience tribulation (2 Peter 3:12), let's enter into it with the understanding that God is with us in the fiery trials and will not allow us to be utterly destroyed by them. And after all is said and done, the evidence of our fiery furnace experience will not be singed hairs or smoke-filled clothes but rather the absence of some of the "ropes" that had bound our hands and feet, and the testimony that God was right there with us through it all, from beginning to end (even if we can only see it in hindsight).

But remember that the temptations that come into your life are no different from what others experience. And God is faithful. He will keep the temptation from becoming so strong that you can't stand up against it: "When you are tempted, he will . . . provide a way out so that you can stand up under it" (1 Corinthians 10:13).

We hate it when bad stuff happens to us! I long for heaven where pain, disease, theft, loss, miscarriage, death and goodbyes are only things of the past. But this isn't heaven—it is Earth. And life on this planet is full of "earthy" stuff that hurts and disappoints.

There is no heaven without Earth. I want to go to heaven, so I endure Earth. Life on Earth challenges me and beats up all my human emotions. And life on Earth makes me cynical.

Then I remember a saying of my grandmother's: "Earth is the dressing room, Alex. It's the gettin' ready place. It's not our home." Whatever happens here gets us ready for the next dwelling place.

There's a world of difference between heaven and Earth. Yet there is something that makes them both beautiful. There is something that makes life on Earth tolerable, even in the midst of heartache and sickness and death. That something is the sweet presence of our sovereign God.

The God of heaven stands with me during the fiery trials of life. We are never alone! Not even in suffering. How can we suffer alone when God is with us? How can he forget us when he is standing with us in the fire?

Therefore our suffering is never wasted!

And the sovereign God who created human beings out of dust, will create order out of our chaos, and will make sense of our suffering, and has earned our trust in the midst of anxiety, and will convert our pain into something glorious.

Earth is where my ropes are burned so that I am prepared to walk about heaven. God will redeem our broken, useless pieces into something of value—to him and to us.

> But he knows where I am going. And when he has tested me in a fire, he will pronounce me innocent.
> (Job 23:10 NLT)

12

I Can See Clearly Now

In chapter eight, we met a couple of Jesus' disciples heading to Emmaus—even though Jesus had told them to go to Galilee. I like to call this "the route we take when God ticks us off."

But Jesus shows up. He doesn't wait until they come to their senses. He doesn't wait until they see the light. He follows his wayward disciples and tracks them down while they are recounting the sad events of the past week: Betrayal and denial. A trial. Public humiliation. And Jesus was crucified—*crucified!* How can this be? He spoke truth. He worked miracles. He made promises.

JESUS LISTENS

Jesus played it cool as he gently broke up this little pity party.

> He asked them, "What are you discussing together as you walk along?"
>
> They stood still, their faces downcast. One of them, named Cleopas, asked him, "Are you only a visitor to Jerusalem and do not know the things that have happened there in these days?" (Luke 24:17-18)

Every time I read this passage, I fall more in love with Jesus! Jesus should've been upset. Jesus should've been hurt. Jesus should've been vengeful. But Jesus was concerned. And he went to find his wayward friends on the road to Emmaus. Emmaus was their getaway destination.

Here we see that Jesus didn't catch up with these men in order to give them a good tongue-lashing. I think he came to let them vent and to reroute their trip.

"What's up? Why do you look so preoccupied?"

This was just what the disciples needed.

"Are you a stranger? Haven't you heard . . . ? Where have you been?

"Our world has been turned upside down, and now we have to rethink our future, our careers . . . our faith.

"He was so convincing. He was so impressive. He had so much potential. We had hoped that Jesus was the Chosen One—but he died and left us here all alone in this hostile world. That's all!"

When you first read this passage, you feel great compassion for these disappointed men; they must be heartbroken over losing their friend and Savior. However, as you look closer at the passage, you can't help but wonder what they're really mourning: Jesus' death or the death of their own aspirations? Maybe both. . . . What a day!

It's amazing how Jesus just let them vent. What security he has in his sovereignty and authority! I discussed this passage with a good friend who is a psychologist. He commented that this is classic psychotherapy: asking open-ended questions and allowing people to hear their own hearts, their own biases and their own immaturity.

Jesus is a Wonderful Counselor!

He knew what the men were thinking, but he wanted them to voice their pain. How could he offer them comfort if they never fully acknowledged how much they hurt? How could he offer them a better perspective if they never acknowledged their self-centeredness? How could he send them into the utmost parts of the world as witnesses if they refused believe that his death and resurrection were necessary?

Jesus let them have their say as he patiently waited for them to take a breath.

JESUS SPEAKS

Then Jesus spoke up:

"How foolish you are, and how slow of heart to believe all that the prophets have spoken! Did not the Christ have to suffer these things and then enter his glory?" And beginning with Moses and all the Prophets, he explained to them what was said in all the Scriptures concerning himself. (Luke 24:25-27)

Jesus vented too. Not because of his own selfish ambition, but because of the disciples' selfish ambition—because they didn't listen to anything he had said to them. In fact, they had never really *followed* him. They followed what they thought he was saying, because they put personal gain above the big picture, and because the Father's plan for Jesus' life was just as much a threat to these disciples' egos as it had been for the men who crucified him.

Ouch!

These men weren't merely lamenting their crucified friend. They were lamenting their failed future careers and popularity.

But Jesus showed up to dry their tears and open their eyes. Jesus rebuked the men for what they didn't believe. Then he taught them what they didn't know: God's plan for his life. From the writings of Moses through all the prophets, Jesus took time to lead a small group

Bible study right in the middle of the street—on the road to Emmaus.

And the men did a U-turn.

Perhaps Jesus quoted Isaiah 53:3-8:

He was despised and rejected by men,
    a man of sorrows, and familiar with suffering.
Like one from whom men hide their faces
    he was despised, and we esteemed him not.

Surely he took up our infirmities
    and carried our sorrows,
yet we considered him stricken by God,
    smitten by him and afflicted.
But he was pierced for our transgressions,
    he was crushed for our iniquities;
the punishment that brought us peace was upon him,
    and by his wounds we are healed.
We all like sheep have gone astray,
    each of us has turned to his own way;
and the LORD has laid on him
    the iniquity of us all.

He was oppressed and afflicted,
    yet he did not open his mouth;
he was led like a lamb to the slaughter,
    and as a sheep before her shearers is silent,
    so he did not open his mouth.
By oppression and judgment he was taken away.
    And who can speak of his descendants?
For he was cut off from the land of the living;
    for the transgression of my people he was stricken.

Or Zechariah 12:10: "And I will pour out on the house of David and the inhabitants of Jerusalem a spirit of grace and supplication. They will look on me, the one they have pierced, and they will mourn for him as one mourns for an only child, and grieve bitterly for him as one grieves for a firstborn son."

Wow! The Word of God is like a two-edged sword (Hebrews 4:12). What a gentle Savior! He can rebuke you and restore you in the same breath.

Why do we doubt him?

Why do we rush him?

Why do we run and hide from him?

BEING HONEST WITH JESUS

Jesus didn't explain his truth until Cleopas and the other disciple first told their truth: "We're ticked off at Jesus! He let us down! We deserved better! We gave him our best years."

And guess what? Jesus didn't freak out! Jesus didn't shrivel up at their disappointment. And he won't shrivel up at ours either.

Why do we keep from venting with him? Isn't it obvious that he values honest dialogue?

Our suffering is strange to us; hence we fail to recognize its true worth. A Jesus who permits suffering is strange to us as well; hence we fail to recognize him and the worth of his plan for our lives. We despise suffering and attempt to pray it, *and him,* away.

SEEING JESUS

It is not very curious to me that these disciples did not recognize Jesus on this road. It is more intriguing to me that they had served with him for three years yet never recognized him. Why would they recognize him now? They hadn't up to this point.

The disciples were so sure that God's plan did not involve Jesus' death that they couldn't recognize Jesus as they walked and talked with him. They were face to face with God's answer to all their problems and couldn't see beyond their own thwarted aspirations. When we try to perceive God's plan via a selfish perspective, we fail to recognize Christ as well.

An unrecognized Jesus is an inconvenient Jesus.

The Bible is not only an account of the incarnate Word of God living among us. It is an account of people's perception of who Jesus ought to be, who Jesus ought to be associated with, what day Jesus ought to perform miracles on, how he ought to behave, how he ought to train leaders, how he ought deal with Caesar, and how he ought to live and ought to die.

But the intriguing stranger on the road taught the Scriptures with real authority. Cleopas and the other disciple seemed to have been very interested in his lesson. They listened attentively. Perhaps this was the first time they had heard the gospel with unselfish ears.

Something about this stranger was compelling, soothing and reassuring. They were nearing Emmaus, and Jesus, finishing his lesson, acted as if he was going to go further. But the disciples begged him to stay with them (Luke 24:28-29), essentially saying: "No! You can't leave now. You've made more sense than anyone these past few days. It is not our custom to allow visitors to travel alone after dark. Come with us, please."

We see a little of the character and hospitality of these disciples. Their dreams were dashed, and yet they found it in their hearts to be kind to this stranger. They embraced the stranger, and he saved their lives, their ministries and their broken hearts.

What is this strange object in our lives called suffering? I think it is the Father's ability—even his willingness—to teach us deep truths in the midst of hardship. It is hard for us to believe that God would stoop low enough to use our disappointment, fears and selfish ambition in order to redirect our energy. But if we learn to embrace what is strange or unfamiliar to us, we may find our lives saved as well.

Something interesting happened at the house, awakening the dejected disciples to their senses: "When he was at the table with them, he took bread, gave thanks, broke it and began to give it to them. Then their eyes were opened and they recognized him, and he disappeared from their sight" (Luke 24:30-31).

Was there better lighting inside the house? Did they finally look up to get a good glimpse of his eyes? Was it the way he prayed over the bread? Was it the way he broke the bread?

Or was it the way he handed the bread to them, just as he did when he fed the four thousand? He could have done that miracle all by himself, but he had wanted the disciples to participate with him: "He told the crowd to sit down on the ground. When he had taken the seven loaves and given thanks, he broke them and gave them to his disciples to set before the people, and they did so. They had a few small fish as well; he gave thanks for them also and told the disciples to distribute them" (Mark 8:6-7).

The breaking of bread had always been a partnership between Jesus and his disciples. It wasn't the same with all the disciples scattered, hidden and hopeless without Jesus. This time Cleopas and the other disciple were the famished crowd, and Jesus was again performing a bread miracle.

Or perhaps Jesus' actions reminded them of the very last meal they had had with him, when he washed their feet and broke bread with them, saying: "I am the living bread that came down from heaven. If anyone eats of this bread, he will live forever. This bread is my flesh, which I will give for the life of the world" (John 6:51).

It was Jesus! They finally got it! He had given hints all along—but very few had listened closely enough to catch those hints.

Their eyes were opened. And he had come looking for them just as he had come for the wayward Peter.

What a good shepherd. They didn't understand Jesus' nature, but he knew theirs. They didn't know where Jesus was, but he knew where they were. And when they couldn't get to him, he got to them. "They asked each other, 'Were not our hearts burning within us while he talked with us on the road and opened the Scriptures to us?'" (Luke 24:32).

What an epiphany! "We should've known it! His words were so powerful and so soothing."

Within the hour, the AWOL "soldiers" were back on their posts. Just like that! No court-martial, no dishonorable discharge, no shame on their families, no rumors, no demotion. Complete reinstatement, because Jesus had never dismissed the two. They had dismissed themselves.

Their hearts were warmed. Perhaps this meant that at some point their hearts had become cool toward the faith. These two and their hearts had been separated for nearly five days. All they could feel was numbness. Three years of training and indoctrination, three years of fasting and praying, three years of waiting and seeing, three years of preaching and promises—it had all been dashed in a matter of one cruel day.

And what did Jesus say that warmed their hearts so? He quoted the Word of God to them.

Hardship, disappointment and busyness often take us away from the study of God's Word. We will wither up into the coolness of complacency and fall prey to doubt as well if we are not careful. The Word of God is where Jesus sets the record straight for these two—and for us as well.

The disciples vented to Jesus. Jesus vented to them, and then he took them to the Word of God. For some reason, they were ready to hear truth this time. And they heard something that they hadn't heard in three years—God's plan, rather than their own desires.

It's comforting to know that neither the cold waters of personal ambition nor the strong winds of perceived abandonment were powerful enough to extinguish the heart-flame ignited by the Holy Spirit of God.

The holy fire was rekindled! And boy, did this wildfire spread . . . but only after the told the truth about their disappointment in Jesus.

JESUS BRINGS US INTO COMMUNITY

The community of believers was reestablished:

> They got up and returned at once to Jerusalem. There they found the Eleven and those with them, assembled together and saying, "It is true! The Lord has risen and has appeared to Simon." Then the two told what had happened on the way and how Jesus was recognized by them when he broke the bread.
>
> While they were still talking about this, Jesus himself stood among them and said to them, "Peace be with you." (Luke 24:33-36)

As Cleopas and the other disciple testified to the goodness and reality of the risen Christ, he appeared. He does the same thing when we testify to his goodness with other believers—he appears. Jesus is revealed in community: "For where two or three come together in my name, there am I with them" (Matthew 18:20).

Community is crucial to the Christian faith. Jesus is committed to showing up where community happens.

While Cleopas was describing the mercifulness of the Savior, his gentle-but-stern rebuke and the incredible Bible lesson on Old Testament messianic prophecies, Jesus showed up again and confirmed Cleopas's testimony—and God's holy Word as well.

We cannot allow troubles to separate us from other believers. Jesus often reveals himself and confirms his messages to us through others. Isolation is a deadly enemy to the Christian faith. This reminds me of studying animal kingdoms in middle school and learning how the strong lions picked off the zebra that had wandered off alone, or watching documentaries of wolves that picked off an isolated caribou in the Artic tundra. The predators prefer nonresistant meals, and they like them à la carte. Therefore, they seek out the sickly animals and the loners.

I think our enemy operates in a similar manner. We are easy prey if we allow our heartaches to separate us from the community that God has chosen to nurture and protect us. Hurt Christians should not travel alone.

God used the Christian community to teach me a theology of suffering.

God used the Christian community to tell me that God was not getting even with me.

God used the Christian community to reach out to me when I was too distrustful of God to reach for him.

God used the Christian community tell me things like "How can God forsake you when your two beautiful daughters are sitting in his presence reminding him of you?"

God used community to pray for me. I could feel currents of love coursing through my body while friends were in a prayer meeting interceding for my wife and me.

And Cleopas and his ministry partner returned to encourage the rest of the community with their new revelation of the Savior.

JESUS REAPPEARS

Jesus then reappeared to the entire group, but the group was horri-fied, "thinking they saw a ghost. He said to them, 'Why are you trou-bled, and why do doubts rise in your minds?'" (Luke 24:37-38).

Jesus invited them to touch his scars and nail holes. He was so willing to convince them of the truth that he ate food just to prove that he wasn't a ghost.

Still, they needed more proof. Jesus took the eleven back to Scrip-ture and said: " 'This is what I told you while I was still with you: Everything must be fulfilled that is written about me in the Law of Moses, the Prophets and the Psalms.' Then he opened their minds so they could understand the Scriptures" (Luke 24:44-45).

They, too, had misunderstood Jesus' previous teachings. The Suf-fering Savior was too hot for them to handle. His suffering meant that they had misunderstood the Father's plan for Jesus' life. And that meant that they had misunderstood Jesus' plan for their lives as well. But Jesus opened their minds to truth, and their attitudes changed as a result.

Jesus presents truth. It is our job to hear it, believe it, and act on it boldly and faithfully.

YOUR JOURNEY TO JESUS

Your life matters to God. The hairs on your head are numbered, meaning the most minute and mundane details of your existence are of importance to him. You are never far from God's heart—ever!

Do what you must in order to process your pain: kick, yell, cry, shake your fists, throw things and/or get counseling. But you have too much living to experience to just sit there. Remember, the joy and power of resurrection comes after the pressure of Gethsemane and the lonely sting of Calvary.

I am sure that seeing Jesus writhing in pain in Gethsemane was tough for the disciples to observe. Likewise, I am sure that your friends, relatives or spiritual leaders would love to see you "just get over it"—but you can't do it for them. You have to do it for yourself and for God. You have to wrestle and fight the good fight of faith until you only have strength to surrender and say "Yes, Lord. Have your way. I trust you."

The goodness and mercy of the Lord will follow you all the days of your life. Jesus was able to track down Peter, Cleopas and Doubting Thomas in their darkest hours. He knew their limits, their needs and their whereabouts! He knows yours as well.

God is currently pursuing you fervently—you just probably can't "see" him yet. I pray that you will be receptive to the revelation of his love for you. I pray that your dashed dreams will cause you to seek his dreams for your life. And I pray that you will have the boldness to reply honestly when he asks you, "Why are you sad?" I believe that God wants to heal you of the guilt you feel for being so angry with him, as much as he wants to heal your pain. Let him do both. He can. He longs to. He loves you.

Long ago the Lord said to Israel: "I have loved you, my people, with an everlasting love. With unfailing love I have drawn you to myself" (Jeremiah 31:3 NLT).

PRAYER OF TRANSFORMATION

Now glory be to God! By his mighty power at work within us, he is able to accomplish infinitely more than we would ever dare to ask or hope. (Ephesians 3:20 NLT)

Dear Jesus,

Your life, death, resurrection and ascension have drastically changed world history. I want these truths to drastically change my personal history—my present—and my future as well.

When I think of you in Gethsemane, I stagger at your love for your people, as well as your obedience to our Father's will. I now realize that you understand pain, humiliation, false accusations, fair-weathered-friendships, fickle fans, jealous backbiters, rejection, loneliness, heart-ache and death! You understand me.

Thank you for living to make intercession for us. It's working today! I therefore resolve to live by your power and not my own. I further resolve to seek the Father's plan, just as you did. And I also promise to demonstrate Satan's defeat in every aspect of my life—just as you have instructed your children. And because you defeated Satan and returned us back to our rightful place in God—we hail you, Jesus! Your life frees us to sing and live. Amen!

13

MY TRIBUTE

I must admit that I almost omitted this chapter from the book. I wanted to be careful to not appear to imply that God has rewarded me with a wonderful daughter for my good behavior. I want to be really sensitive to the hurts of my fellow sojourners. Having said that, I realize that I don't want to rob the Lord of much-deserved honor for his faithfulness to Jackie and me, either. So here goes . . .

I call this chapter my tribute to fatherhood, because after many years of struggling with the loss of my daughters, the Lord finally gave me one. Thank you, Jesus! Catherine Alexis Victorias Gee was born December 2, 1996, weighing in at one pound, eight ounces. She gave us all a real scare, but after a 112-day hospital stay, she was released. Local newspapers, television stations and radio stations carried the story of her homecoming.

Rather than trying to write another chapter, I've decided to just share my personal journal entries, e-mails, essays and reflections on the joys of fatherhood.

SECOND CERCLAGE

September 6, 1996

Jackie is thirteen-weeks pregnant today. Presently I sit in the waiting room of the surgery and care center with Jackie's mom, sister and two nephews. They have just taken Jackie back to operate on her cervix and place a cerclage around it. This is Jackie's second such surgery, the last was in the spring of 1993.

It's hard to believe that we are here again! The loss of Alexis in 1993 was so devastating, especially after undergoing all of the medically precautionary measures that were prescribed to us. Jackie and I had actually become comfortable with the idea that we may never become parents. We had resolved to committing ourselves fully to the work of the ministry and actively participating in the lives of our nieces, nephews, young cousins, godchildren and children in our church. We actually felt really good about our decision and comforted our families with the fact that we were doing fine.

It's so ironic; Jackie and I decided to sneak off and celebrate our eighth wedding anniversary in Chicago (June 18). This year our anniversary fell on a Tuesday, but we decided to begin celebrating on that Sunday, Father's Day. I started off my day thinking about fatherhood—the father I never really knew, the stepfather I never knew intimately and the father I would never become. I did something that I have never done in my thirty-two years of being a son— I called my biological father to wish him happy Father's Day. As an act of courtesy, I presume, my father wished me a happy Father's Day in return. "I'm not a father," I sternly reminded my father. Was he so far removed from my life that he'd forgotten that I had been denied fatherhood twice? "I know what happened in the past, but that doesn't stop you from being a father, so . . . happy Father's Day!" I couldn't believe it, after thirty-two years missing birthdays, track meets, award presentations, my high school and college graduations, newspaper articles and even my wedding—my father actually said something that brought me great comfort. Father's Day 1996 would start off a happy one this year and would end up an even happier one as Jackie would conceive that very night. . . .

Doctor William Koller just came out to inform me that the procedure went well and that I would be able to see Jackie in a half hour or so. One huge hurdle has now been jumped. I feel really good and have a great deal of peace of mind. Dr. Koller said that Jackie's cervical cultures showed that the antibiotics are working and there is no infection present in the cervix. This is particularly good news since the prognosis of the last pregnancy was that infection set in after the cerclage was put in and ruptured the membranes, which caused premature labor and delivery. Jackie and I are in an ideal state of mind and spirit. When this baby comes, we will celebrate our Year of Jubilee. And if we should lose this child, and I don't believe we will, we realize that it does not mean that God is angry with us. Jackie and I can't lose this time! Whatever the outcome, we are already victorious.

IT'S A GIRL

December 15, 1996

Dear Friends and Prayer Partners,
I haven't talked with you in a while, so I wanted to update you on what is new with me. You may or may not know by now: Jackie gave birth to Catherine Alexis three weeks ago (12/2). Catherine Alexis (Lexi) was fifteen weeks early and weighed only 1 lb. 8 oz. Her name means "representative of pure victory!" She is our third child but our first to live. She is our Christmas present from the Lord.

To say that Lexi's arrival was highly unusual would be an under-statement. Jackie suffered an abruption, which means that the pla-centa was tearing away from the uterus, on top of labor pains. In fact, the placenta was delivered with the baby. Since Jackie was only twenty-five weeks pregnant, her contractions were not registering on the fetal monitor. The doctor later told us that if they had known that Jackie was in labor they would have given her medicine to stop them (since she showed no sign of infection); however, in hindsight they re-alize that the baby would've died in the process. Praise God for hid-ing the contractions from the doctors!

Jackie was able to hold on until her own doctor got back into town, and he safely delivered our little baby. We almost needed a C-section because the baby was coming too fast and had decreasing heart tones due to Jackie's strong contractions. The doctor had to cut Jackie's cer-vix in order to get the baby here safely, and there was not even enough time for anesthesia! And when the baby was born there was a knot in the umbilical cord—this would've definitely caused prob-lems if this baby had been full term, according to the doctor.

Lexi is doing real well and is expected to be in the hospital until her due date: March! We were told that she would not be able to be fed breast milk (via tube) for two to three weeks, and that she would be on an IV for a while. That was not what God said. The head of neonatology stopped me in the hall on Thursday and told me that they were going to start the baby on breast milk (they have had Jackie pumping and storing milk since delivery)! He called this a "miracle." He went on to say, "I could be secular and call this highly unusual, but my jaw almost hit the ground when I heard that they were putting a three-day-old premature baby on breast milk!" I can't tell you how happy Jackie and I are about this. They took Lexi's IV out on Sunday (12/8), and there has been talk of removing her from the respirator *sometime soon! The doctors say that their department has never had a twenty-five-week premature baby go off the IV and start breast milk in the first week! Ever!*

Jackie is in great spirits and is visiting the baby daily with me. It's tough to love and handle the baby through her incubator; however, it's better than what we've experienced in the past. We are very encouraged and feel the love of God and the love of Christ's body every day. I'll be sure to keep you posted. Next Monday marks the beginning of week four—keep praying with us.

Alex and Jackie

I LAUGHED TILL I CRIED

Dear Lexi,

I heard you cry for the very first time yesterday—and I laughed for the first time in a very, very long time.

You see, your birth was so premature that your lungs hadn't developed fully. When you were born, you weren't able to cry. To be blunt, you couldn't even breathe. The doctors and nurses wouldn't even let your mother and me touch you; they rushed you off to resuscitate you. What's more, your body was so tiny when you were born that you needed lots of help breathing. So you soon had a respirator tube in your mouth, a feeding tube in your nose and occasionally an IV in your navel. And because you had a case of jaundice, your eyes were often blindfolded so the fluorescent lights in your incubator would not harm them.

So when I walked up to your incubator and saw that your respirator tubes were gone, I rejoiced! All of a sudden I heard a sweet, faint little song—and discovered that it was your sweet, faint little voice crying. You squirmed, frowned and waved your tiny fists as you cried. You were clearly upset about something; I realized that you were several weeks old, but this was the first time your daddy had ever heard your voice.

So I laughed and laughed and laughed!

That was nearly two months ago.

Today I heard you laugh for the very first time. It made me cry.

You see, there were so many obstacles to your healthy birth and development: lack of oxygen in the womb; low birth weight, which could have led to brain damage; retina detachment, which could have led to blindness; a breathing disorder, which could have led to cardiac arrest—etc., etc., etc. Your little heel was poked for blood on a daily basis. Your slowly developing lungs were suctioned for mucus almost hourly. Your eyelids were pried open so that the ophthalmologist could take a peek behind your eyeballs to make sure that further damage to your retina wouldn't occur. And a feeding tube was threaded through your nose into your stomach every four or five days. I wondered how all the medical procedures, along with not being able to hold you, rock you or touch you for several weeks, months even, would affect you.

But today you looked beyond all of your struggles, you saw some bright light at the end of a very long tunnel, and you experienced joy. You had endured the pokes and prods of countless specialists and nurses, brain scans, biopsies, transfusions, physical and occupational therapy, inoculations with dosages so large that they were administered via an IV tube and lasted several hours. Notwithstanding, you and your heavenly Father decided that none of those things were strong enough to break your mighty spirit. And in order to openly demonstrate your middle name, Victorias, and your triumph over the incubator, you laughed today—for the very first time. Your entire

little body jiggled like Jell-O as you giggled out loud.
   And I cried and cried and cried!

Love,
Dad

THE DAD POEM

June 11, 2000

Dad!

I love being a dad.

I get to be a herolike role model for my little girl.

I get to observe many of Lexi's firsts.

And being a professional communicator, I love to oohhhh and ahhhh at her new words and phrases.

"Cookie." "Bottle." "Juice." "Bye-bye." "Night-night." "Boo-boo." "Mine!" and "No!" are just a few of the cute things that Lexi has learned to say.

But last night I heard Lexi use a word that I have never used—at least not in the context in which she did.

I have a B.A. from a Big Ten school, the University of Wisconsin-Madison, with a double major in Afro-American history and economics. I am in graduate school. I am an ordained pastor. I have an honorary doctorate in divinity. I preach and lecture all over this country to all kinds of audiences in churches, seminaries, colleges and universities. I have a decent command of the English language and can hold my own in Spanish in a pinch. However, Lexi has mas-

tered a word that makes me cringe when I say it—and melt when I hear it.

"Dad!"

She called me Dad last night.

I love being a dad.

I get to be a herolike role model to my little girl.

I get to observe many of Lexi's firsts—and she gets to observe mine.

GIGGLE

I would like to paint a word portrait of my daughter, Lexi. Here is the canvas on which I wish to draw her:

Joy
Fear
Hope
Legacy
Responsibility

Lost dreams
Dreams come true
Old wounds healed
Pure victory
Fatherlessness
Fatherfulness

If I were asked to paint my daughter in the language of my soul, rather than the language of my intellect, I would use the following "colors":

Lexi is a giggle.

Lexi is too dainty (not to be confused with weak) to be a guffaw.

Lexi is too determined to be a laugh.

Lexi is too strong to be a simple smile.

Lexi is too pure to be a mere grin.

And Lexi is too full of destiny and purpose to be a snicker.

She is a giggle.

I bet you that the Creator giggled when the thought of Lexi first
crossed his mind.

I bet the thought of what she would mean to my wife and me
made him giggle too.

I bet the thought of defeating Satan with such a simple yet in-
trinsically God-sanctioned giggle made him giggle.

I bet he still giggles at his glorious handiwork today.

The doctors giggled as they practiced medicine on such a re-
sponsive and determined baby.

The nurses giggled as Lexi grew.

Her parents giggled as their seed incubated right before their
eyes for 112 days.

Make no mistake—Lexi is not a giggler.

She is a giggle.

She is the outward manifestation of a wild fantasy, curled on the
lips of a curiously pensive father.

Sarah and Abraham called their firstborn Isaac, which means
laughter, because he made them laugh in disbelief.

We should have called Lexi giggle, because she makes us giggle
in disbelief.

She also makes me giggle with belief—and faith.

I giggle because God has restored me.

I giggle because I can breathe again.

I giggle because I can see God and he rests in my sleeping daughter in the nursery next to our bedroom.

I giggle because I can see myself, too, in my daughter.

I giggle because I can.

I giggle because I should . . .

Lexi is not a giggler.

I am!

Lexi is a giggle.

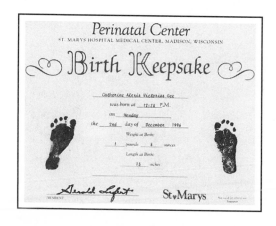

Afterword

Rest in Peace, Victoria and Alexis

Dear Victoria and Alexis,

This chapter is probably the hardest thing I have written in my life. This is the part where I say my kind words and goodbyes to you.

Though I have preached about you and talked openly about your births, I have not fully celebrated your lives or mourned your deaths.

Your deaths represented so much pain and loss of control for me. Your deaths reminded me that your father is so frail. He is so wounded. He is so afraid of life and love and failure. Your deaths sneaked up on me and revealed my brokenness for the entire world to see. My life was never the same after your untimely departures.

I am so sorry.

I am sorry that my memories of you have only been painful.

I am sorry that we met under such grim circumstances.

I am sorry that I can't go near the box with your tiny clothes and pictures in the basement.

And I am sorry that I have not had the courage to put flowers on your tiny graves.

I am so sorry.

I think one of the reasons I love your sister, Lexi, so much is that I had been saving up all that love for my children. She has to put up with all my hugs and kisses all the time. I give her the love I couldn't give you. She gets three times the love. Your mom and I gave her your first names as her middle names, Catherine Alexis Victorias Gee. What a sweet legacy she aptly carries. You'd be so proud of her.

My love for her had dulled me to the pain of your memories, until I sat down to write this book and all the emotions flooded back over my heart.

I need you to know that I am no longer ashamed . . .

of my fatherlessness that caused me to want you so much.

of my losses, because I held you both long enough to love you forever.

And I am a better man and husband and father, because of you.

We believe in a heaven where loved ones are reunited. And I believe that you have beheld the face of God Almighty—with you there, how could he forget me here?

Your mother and sister and I rejoice in knowing that you are not alone; you are with Jesus—and each other.

Know that I can never hug or kiss or play with Lexi without thinking of you.

Thank you for releasing me now to live in peace and courage. I release you to rest in sweet peace as well. My heart is freer than it has been in such a long time. Please know that you both give me two more reasons for loving heaven.

Night-night.

Love,

Daddy

ACKNOWLEDGMENTS

There are so many people who helped me maintain my faith and sanity during the rough periods of my life. I am who I am because of God's grace and Christian community; at Fountain of Life Church we like to call it God's sweet gift of togetherness.

Jackie Gee—my beautiful wife of eighteen years, who knows how to fight a good fight of faith like a tremendously godly woman. I appreciate your faith and stamina. Thank you and Jesus for making me a dad.

Lillian Evans—my deceased grandmother, who taught me as a young boy that following Christ was not for the fainthearted.

Catherine (Lexi) Gee—my wonderful daughter who helps me to understand the Father's love in ways I've never fathomed. You are one of life's sweetest gifts.

Alexandra Gee-Lewis—my lovely niece, who I would visit and hold when I was sad and heartbroken over the loss of my daughters, and feel God's comfort. Thanks for your healing ministry.

Lee Hough—you helped me shape the first and trickiest chapter of this book.

Verline Gee-Fleming—thank you, Mom, for your strong presence in the delivery room those dark nights. Thank you also for our "Loss" poem at the beginning of this book.

Ardenia (Dean) Malone—the best mother-in-law in the world. You moved to Madison, Wisconsin, nine years ago to care for your sick granddaughter and her nervous parents. We appreciate you more than you'll ever know.

Mark Kramer—a true friend who offered me moral support as he sat with me and encouraged me as I worked through the hardest parts of this book, even though he had to meet a deadline for his own book, *Dispossessed: Life in Our World's Urban Slums.* Thank you!

Lilada Gee—my sister, who, after reading my first draft, trashed it and challenged me to write from the heart and not the head. She supported me even as she struggled to meet the deadline for her own book, *I Can't Live Like This Anymore!* Thanks.

Fountain of Life (FOL) Church and staff—my faith community that nurtures, celebrates and affirms me and my family. Thank you for supporting and encouraging my work in the broader church community.

Key FOL Men—especially Patrick, Kevin, Jerome, Brian, Corey, Roberto, Andre, Anthony, Brett, Jim, Chris, Sam and Bill. For years you men have held up my arms like Aaron and Hur did for Moses.

Dr. Steve A. Hayner—a gift to any man's soul! Thank you listening to my ranting and raving about my father issues. You know this story better than anyone. Thank you for being my brother.

Chris Campbell and the Fitchburg Panera Bread Staff—thank you for letting me do so much of my writing in your friendly store.

William Koller M.D. and staff—because you took your time and listened to Jackie's symptoms, and acted accordingly, I have a healthy, beautiful child. Thank you for your medical heroics that Monday morning on December 2, 1996.

John Kenney, M.D., Karen Wiringa, M.D., and staff of St. Mary's Neonatal Intensive Care Unit—thank you for the great care you gave my family. And a special thank you to all the dedicated nurses like Marsha, Diane and Mary Anne (and others), who for 112 days and nights, held, bathed and "lullabied" my daughter when she was too sick for us to care for her.

My Lord—after nearly forty years of having no relationship with my father, you seemingly touched both of our hearts without much warning and are giving us a second chance. My father recently spent Christmas with me and my family. It was our first Christmas holiday together since I was a year old. (This strange gift came out of nowhere just weeks after completing the manuscript for this book.)

And more importantly, thank you Jesus for not walking away when I pushed you away. I can't tell you the joy I have in telling people about your faithfulness. It's time the world learned the truth about the depth of your love for broken people.